AF265888

WOLFEBORO BLESSINGS

Published by Best Seller Publishing®, St. Augustine, FL
Best Seller Publishing® is a registered trademark.
Printed in the United States of America.

ISBN: 978-1-969338-62-5

For more information, please write:
Best Seller Publishing®
1775 US-1 #1070
St. Augustine, FL 32084
or call 1 (626) 765-9750

Visit us online at: www.BestSellerPublishing.org

Book of photos by Helen Fernald

WOLFEBORO BLESSINGS

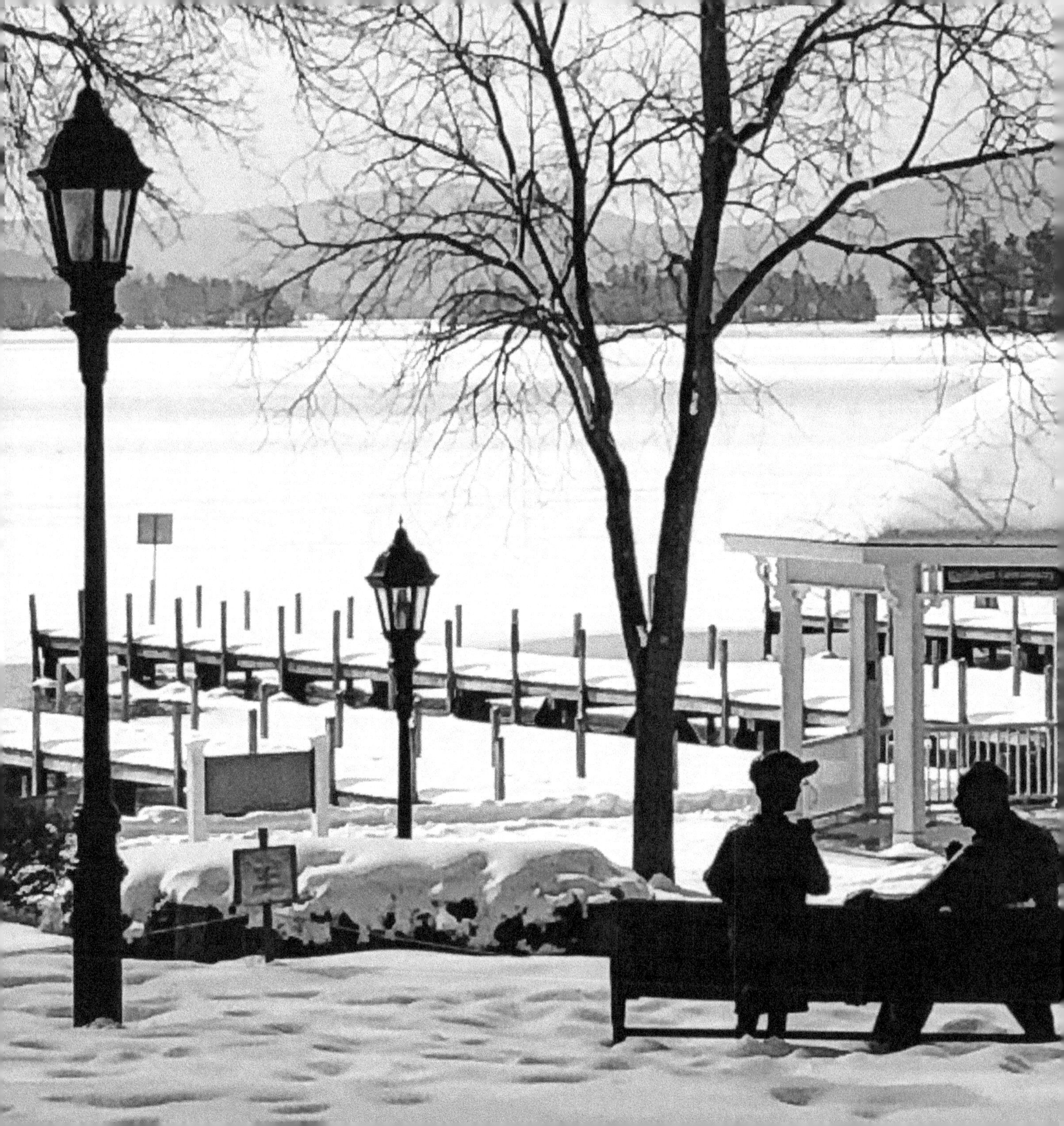

May this new day
bring you peace

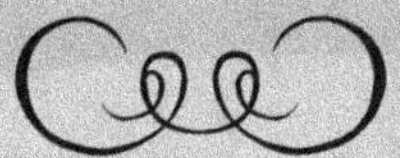

May winter's beauty astound you

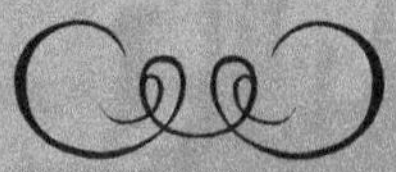

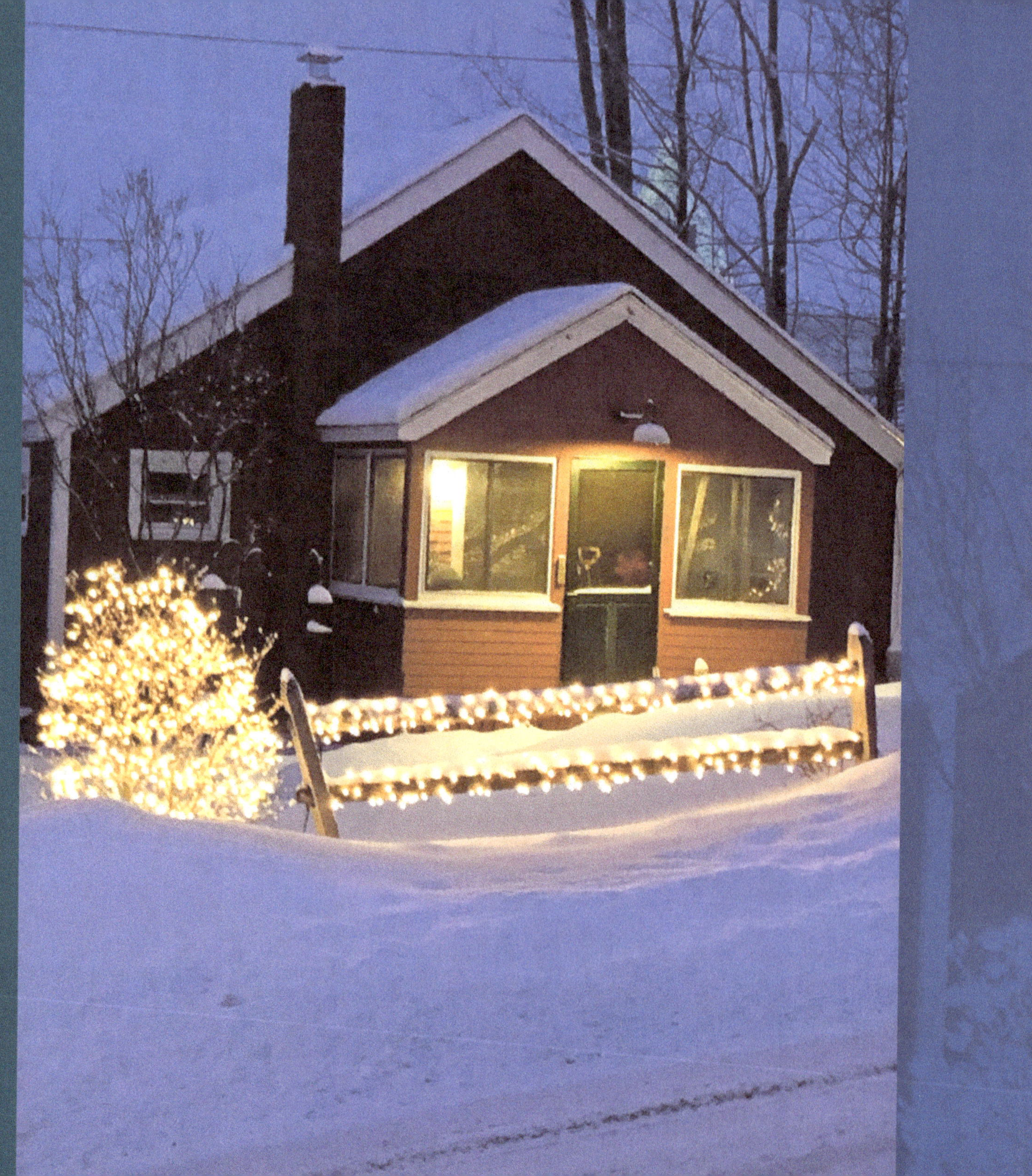

May you feel cozy
and warm today

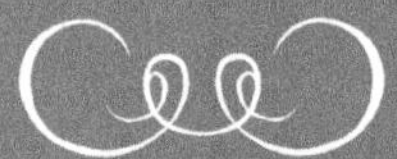

May this January sunrise illumine your day

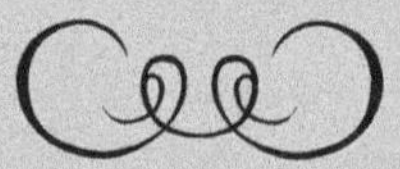

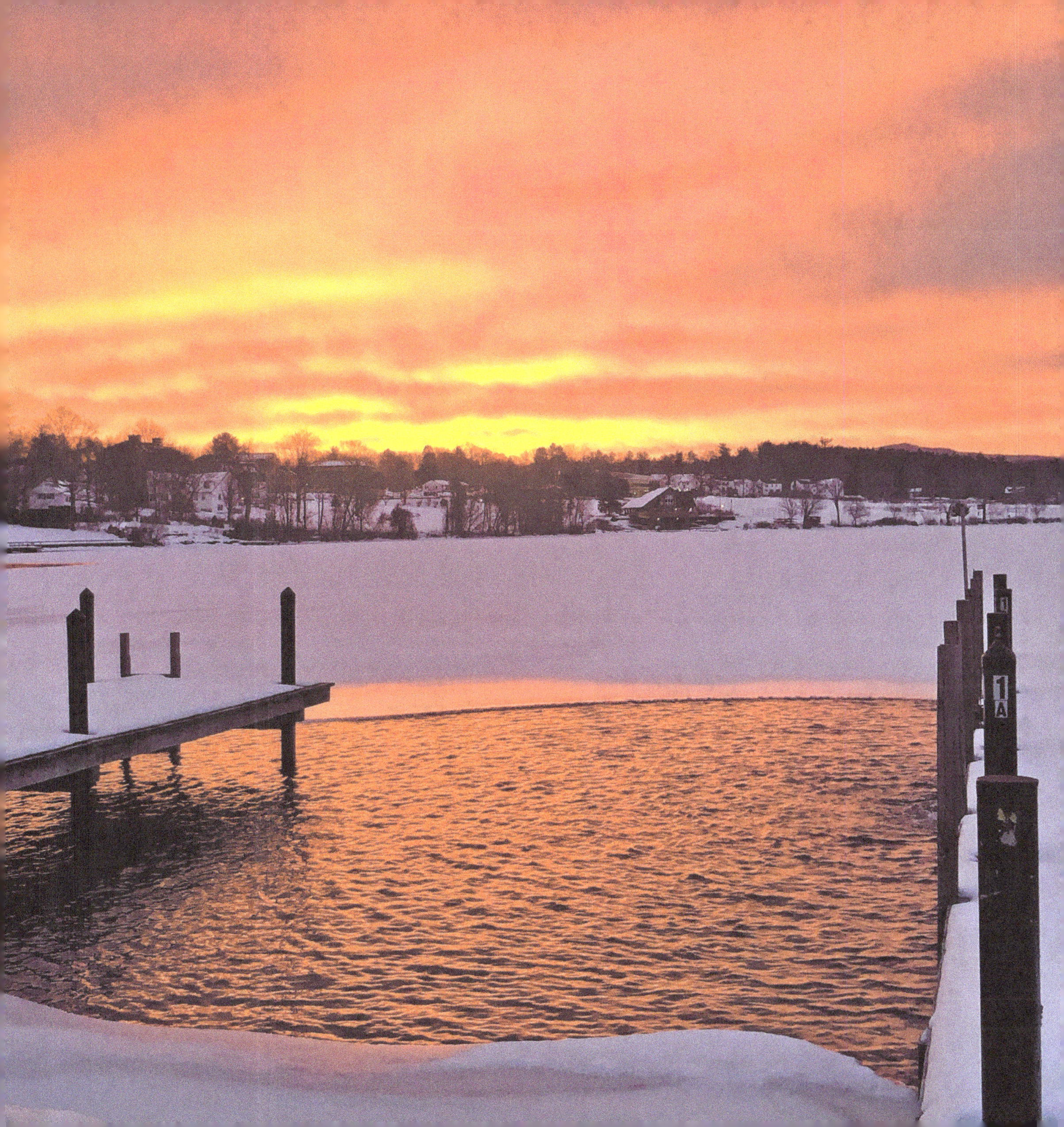

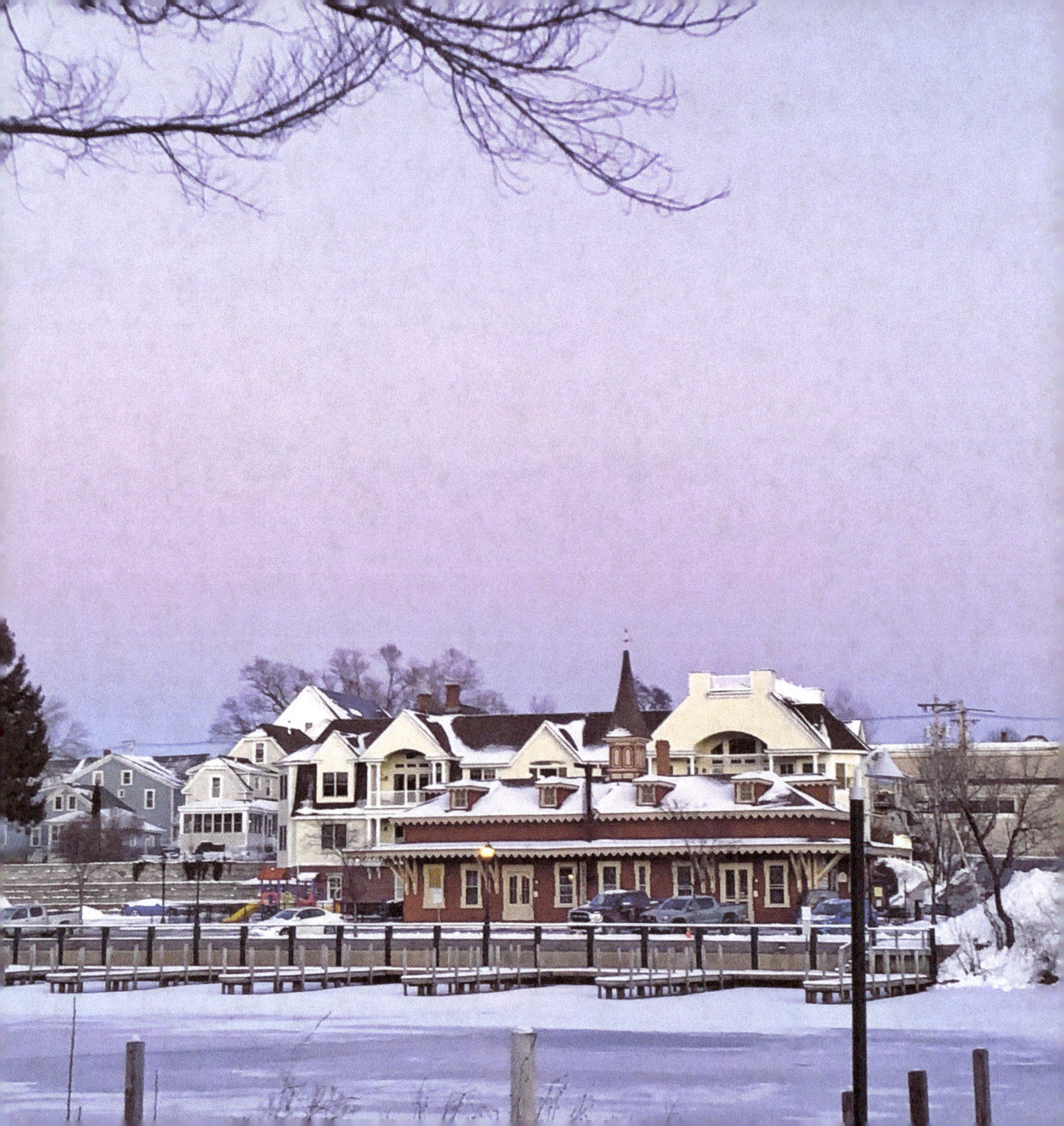

May calmness settle
over you today

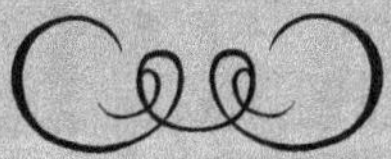

May gentleness walk
with you today

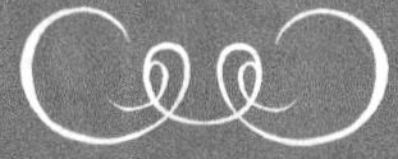

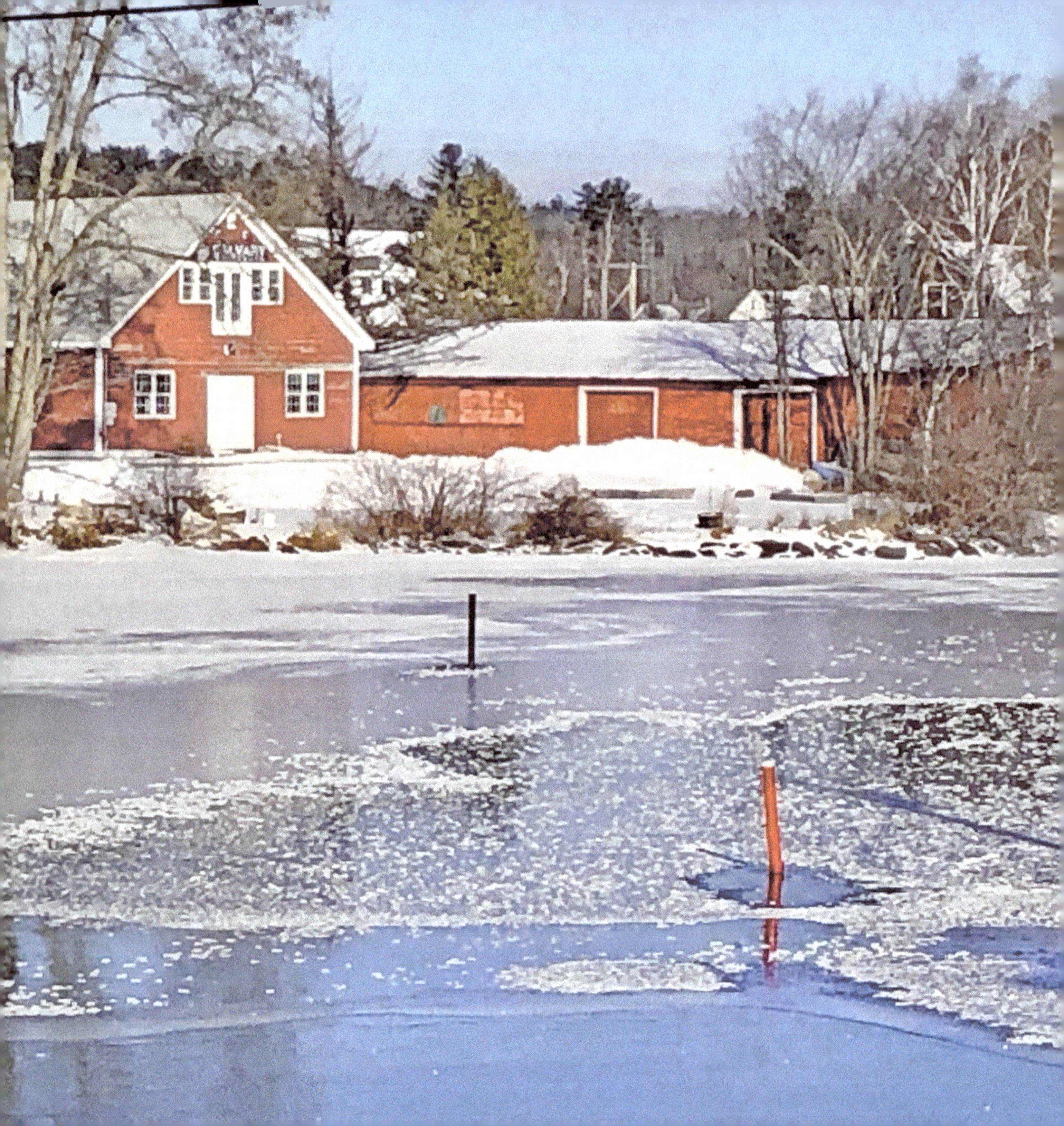

May February's artistry delight you

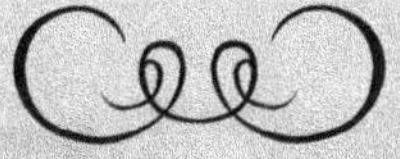

May your heart be
at peace on this day

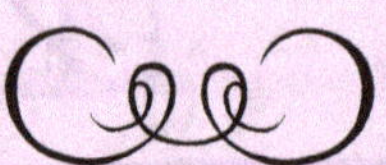

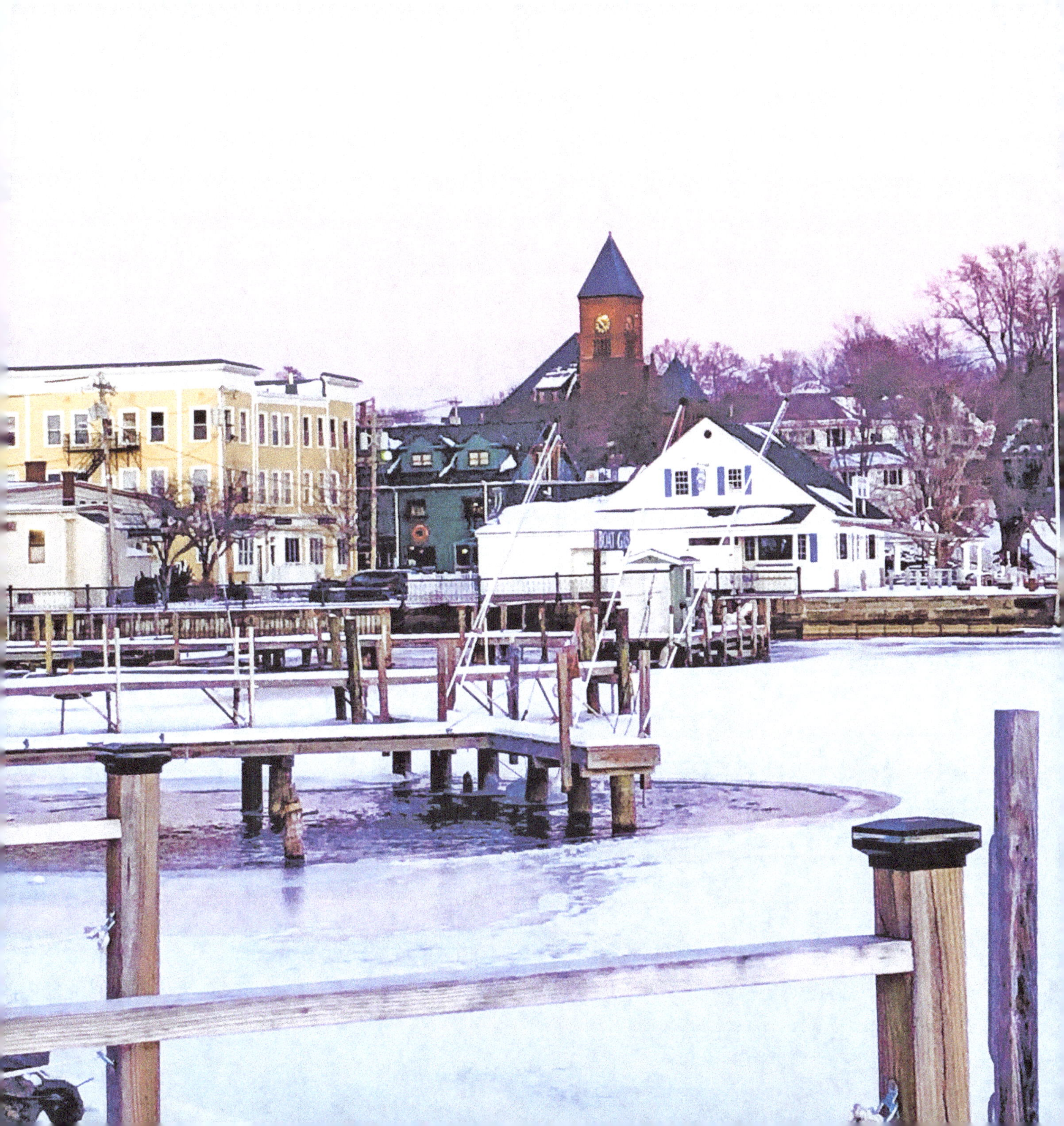
BOAT GAS

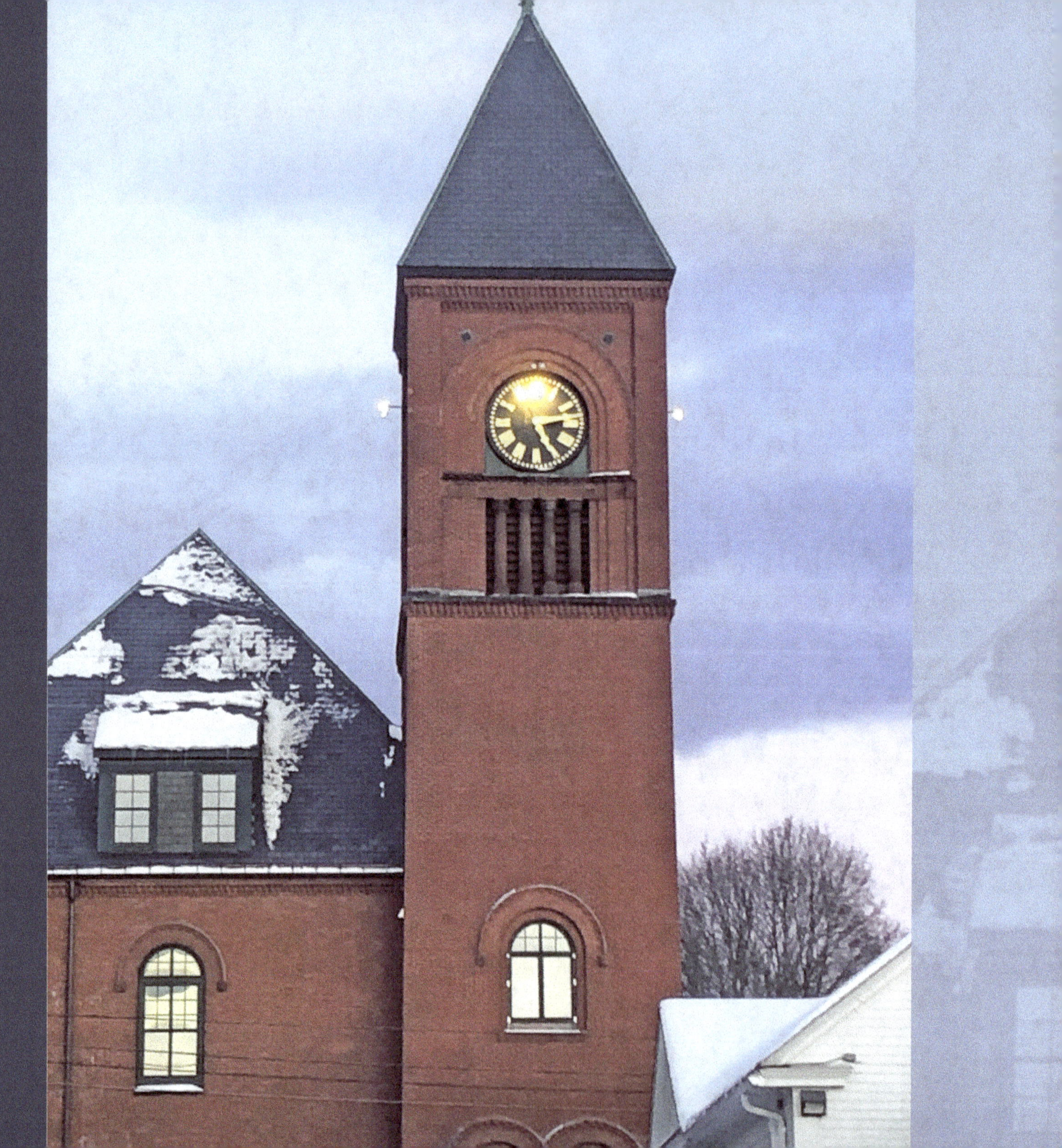

May you always find time to enjoy life

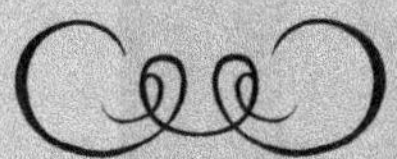

May the magic of
this sunset enchant you

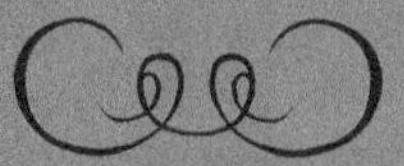

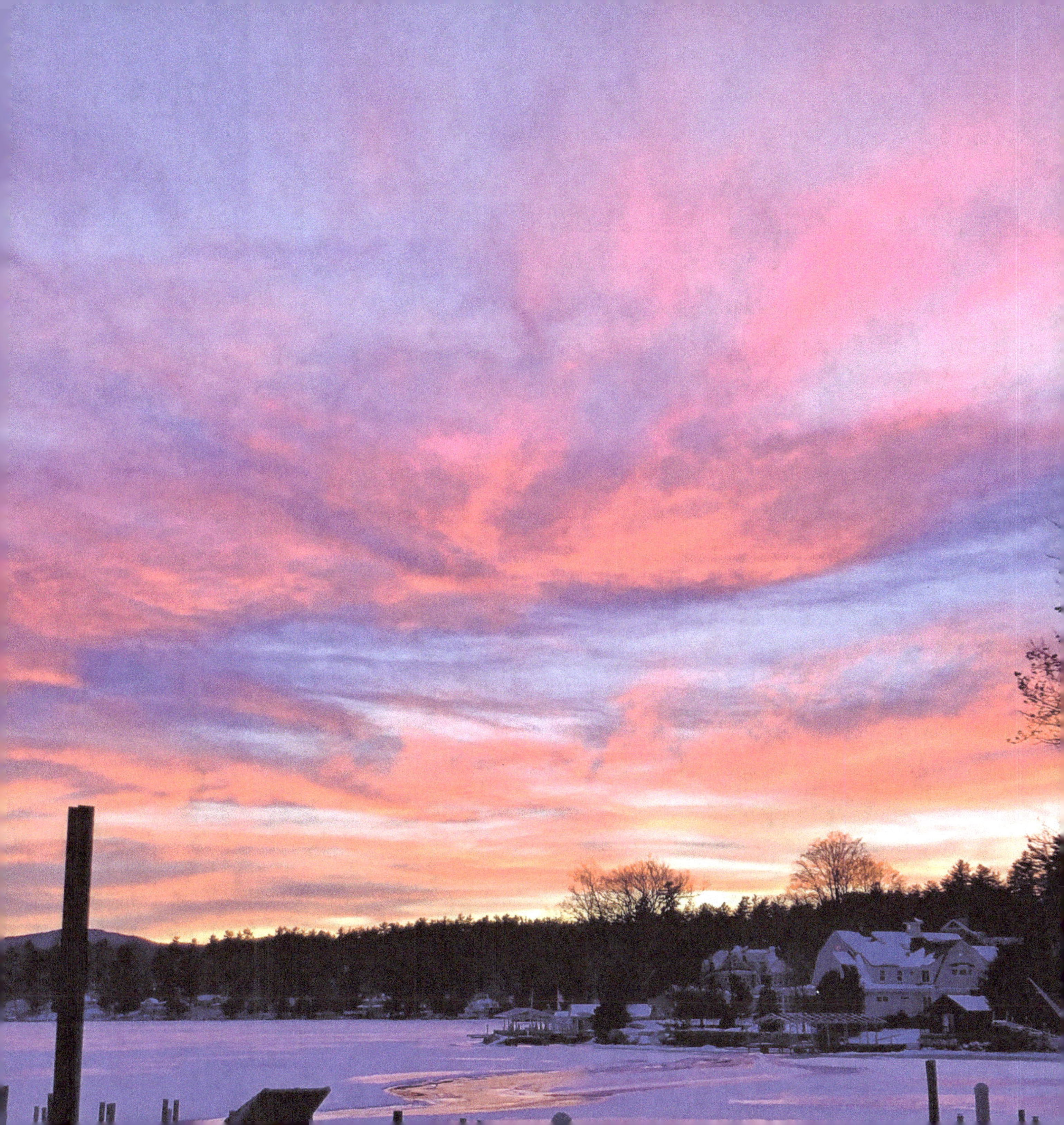

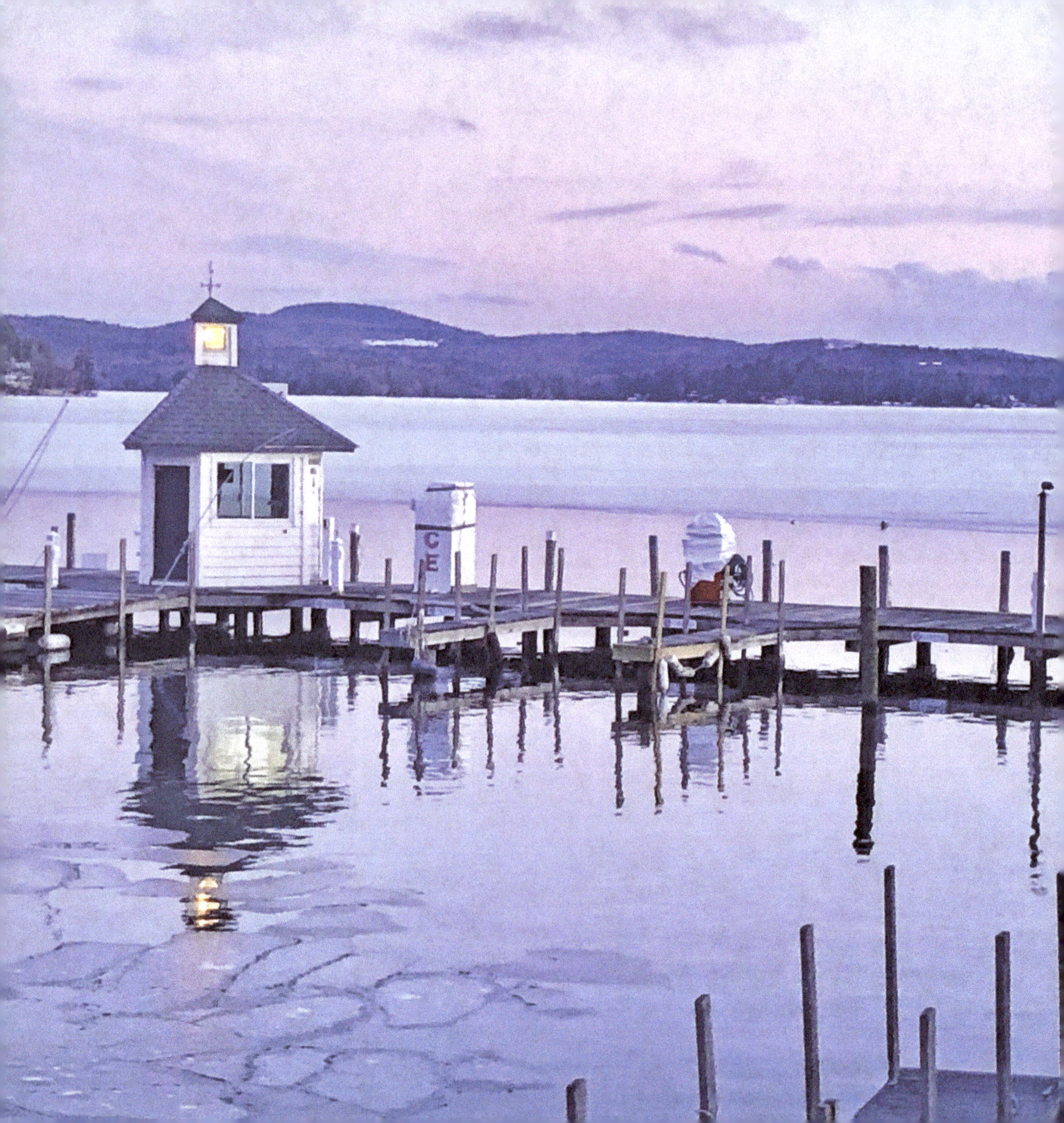

May your spirit
be restful today

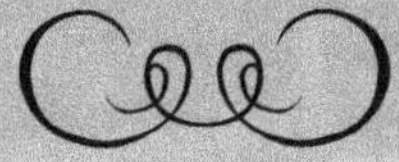

May happy memories dance
in your heart today

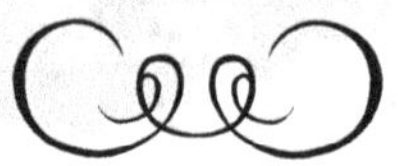

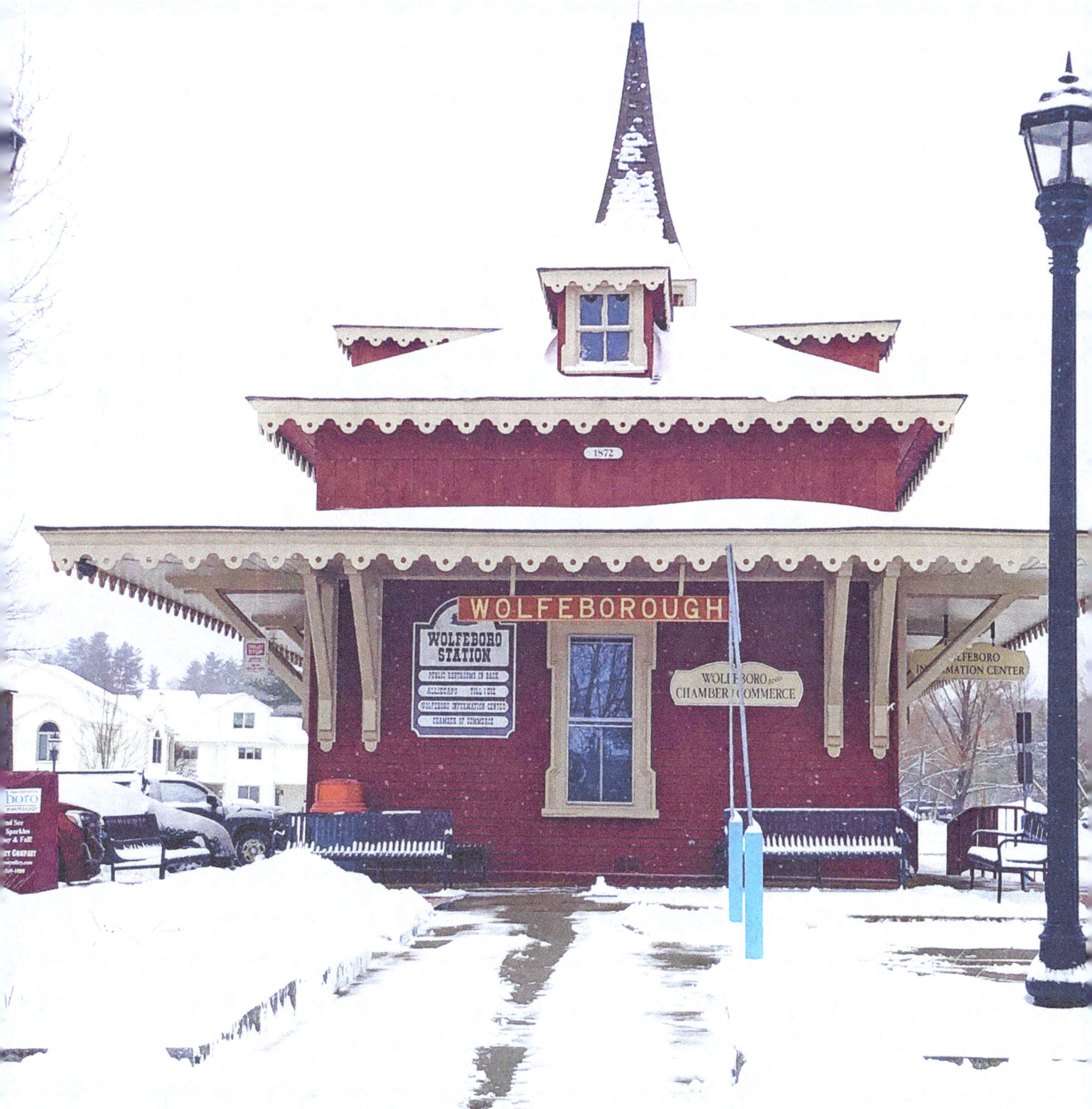

1872
WOLFEBOROUGH
WOLFEBORO STATION
PUBLIC RESTROOMS IN BACK
WOLFEBORO INFORMATION CENTER
CHAMBER OF COMMERCE
WOLFEBORO
CHAMBER OF COMMERCE
WOLFEBORO INFORMATION CENTER
STOP

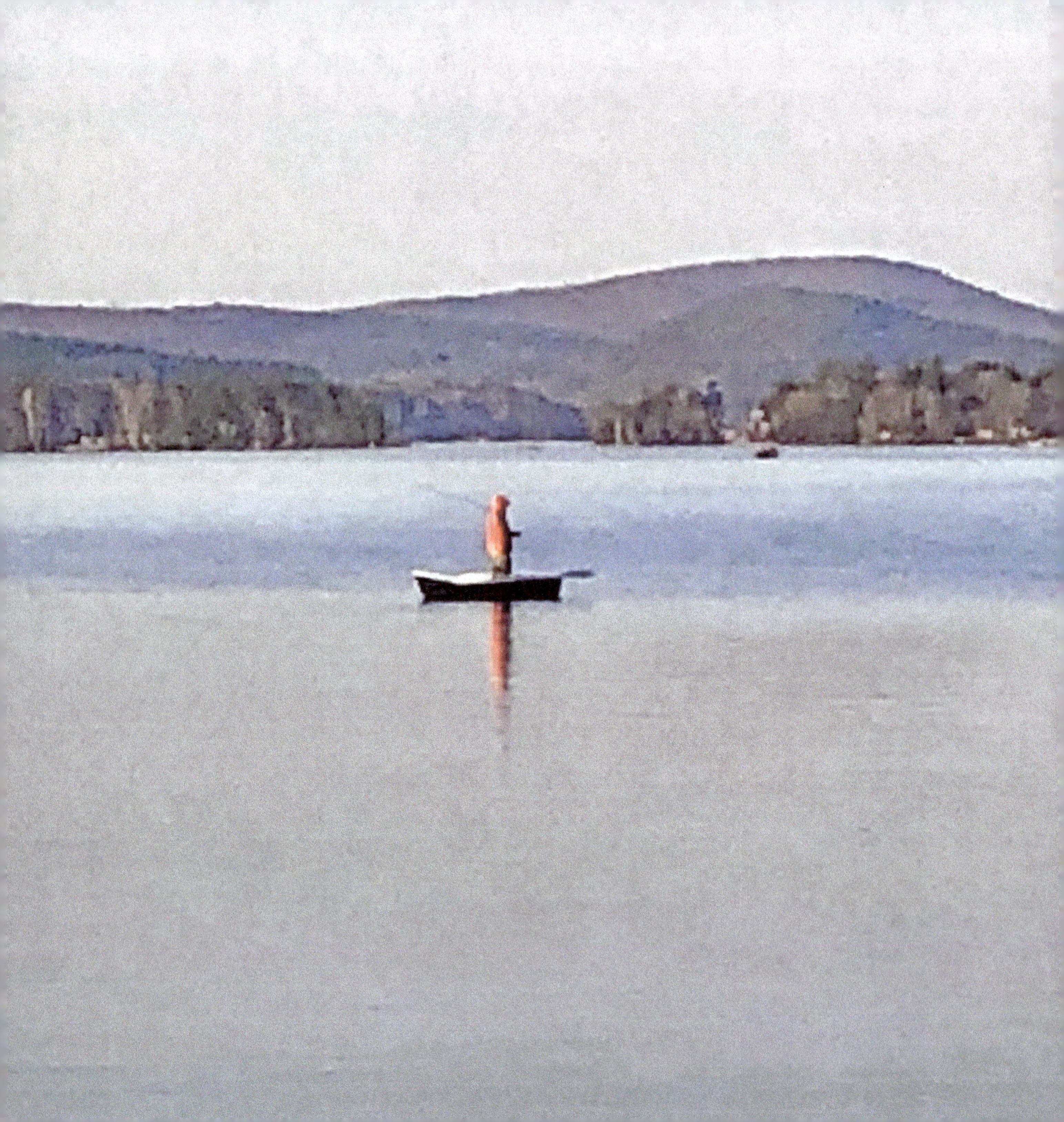

May spring's silence
beckon to you

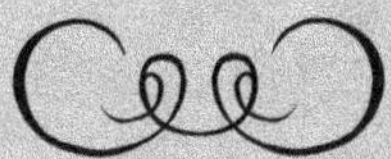

May joy fill
your heart today

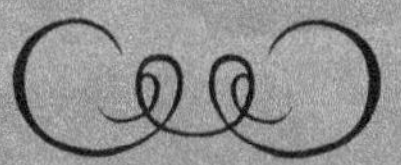

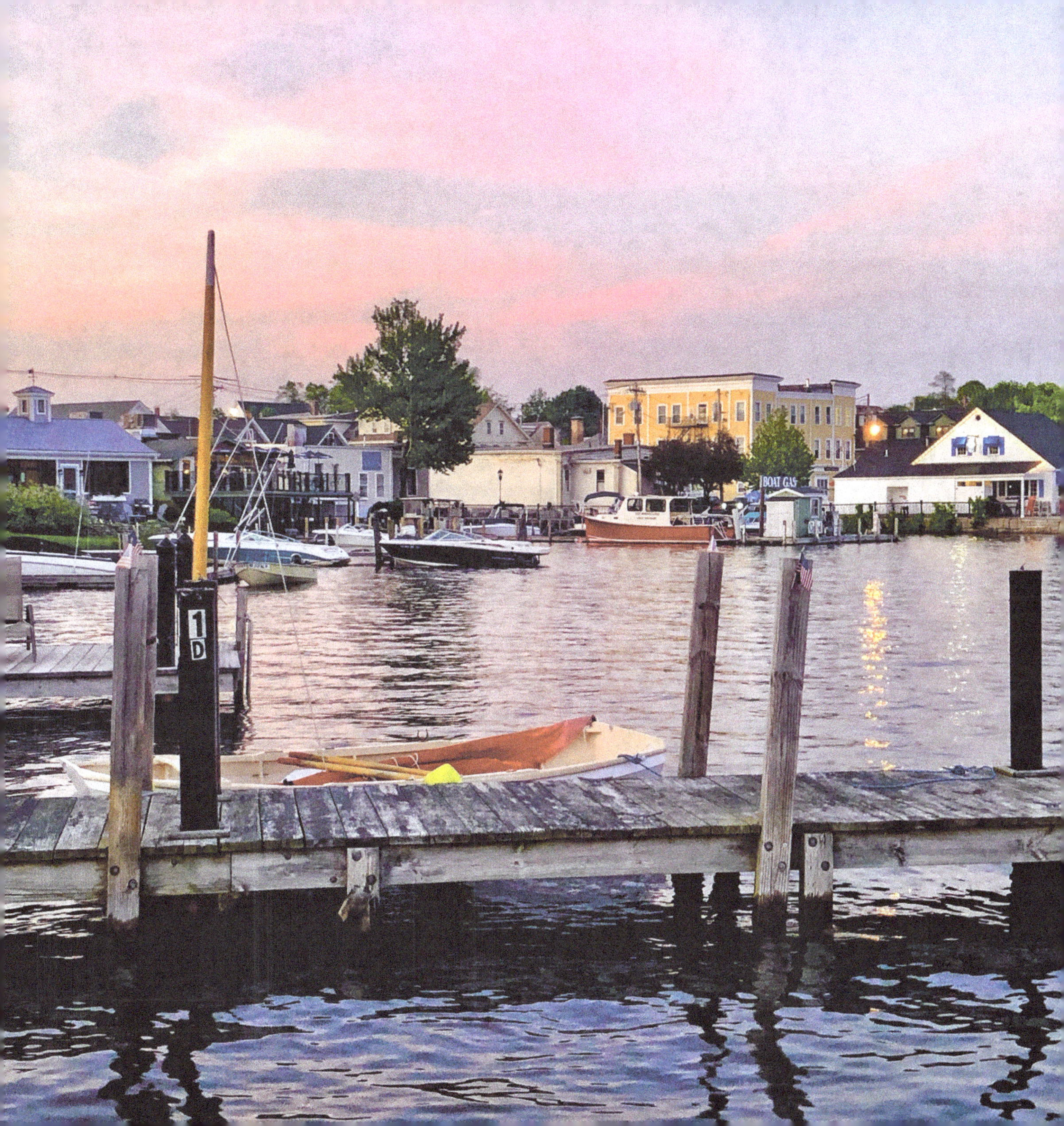

1
D
BOAT GAS

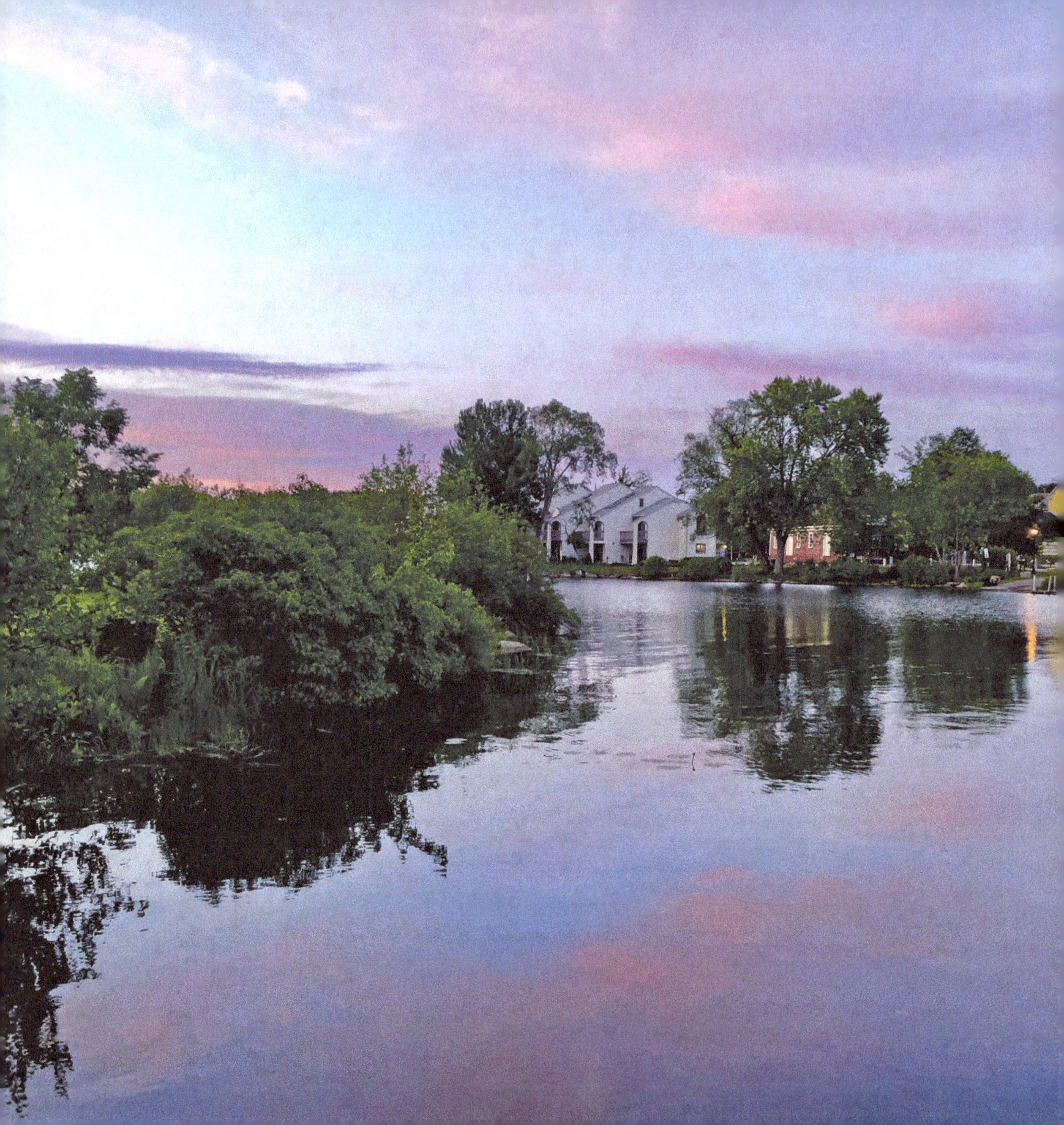

May you pause to soak
in the beauty of this day

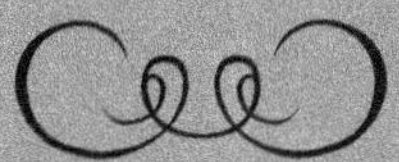

May you take a moment
to reflect on your joy

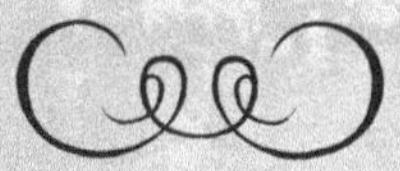

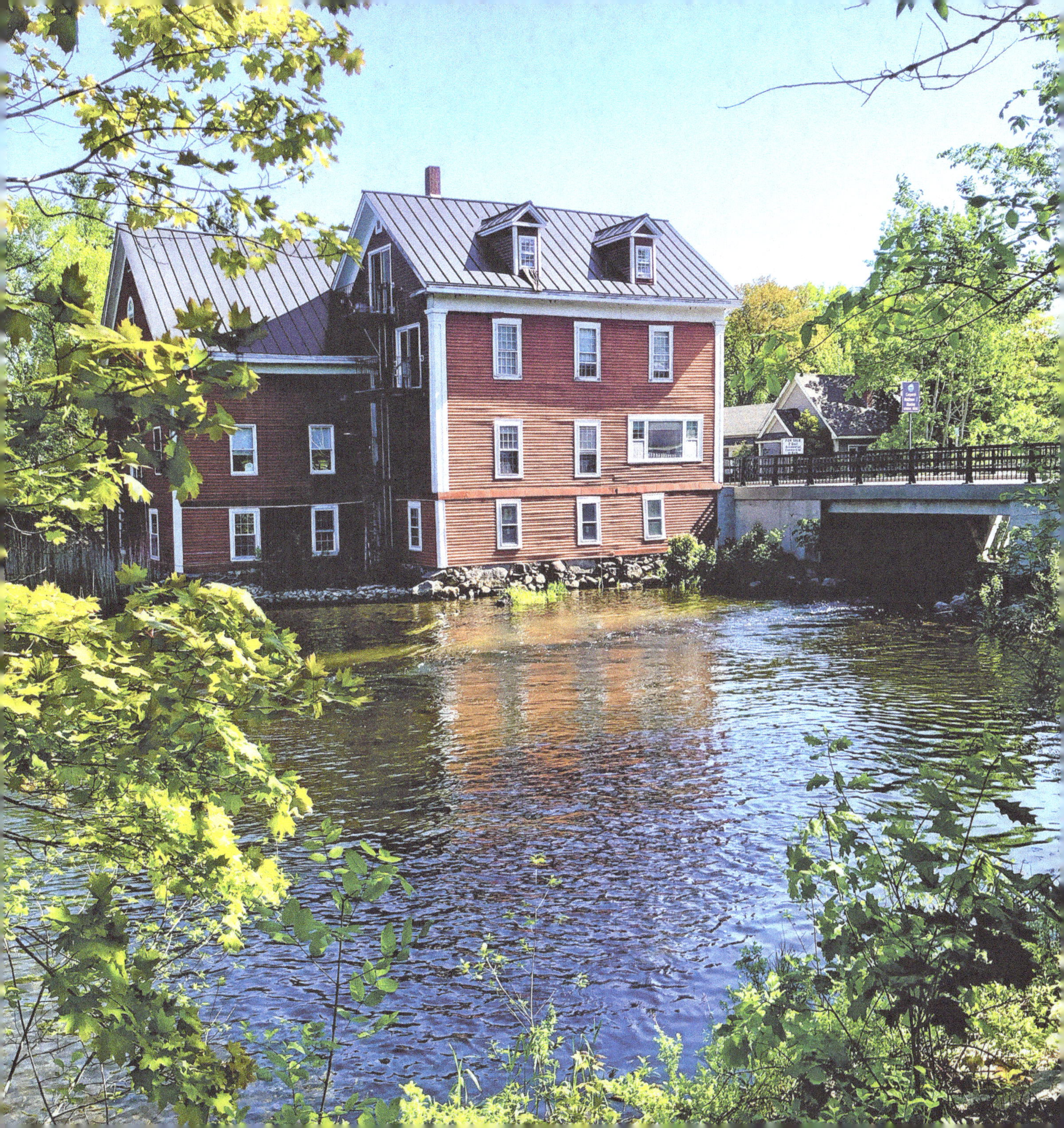

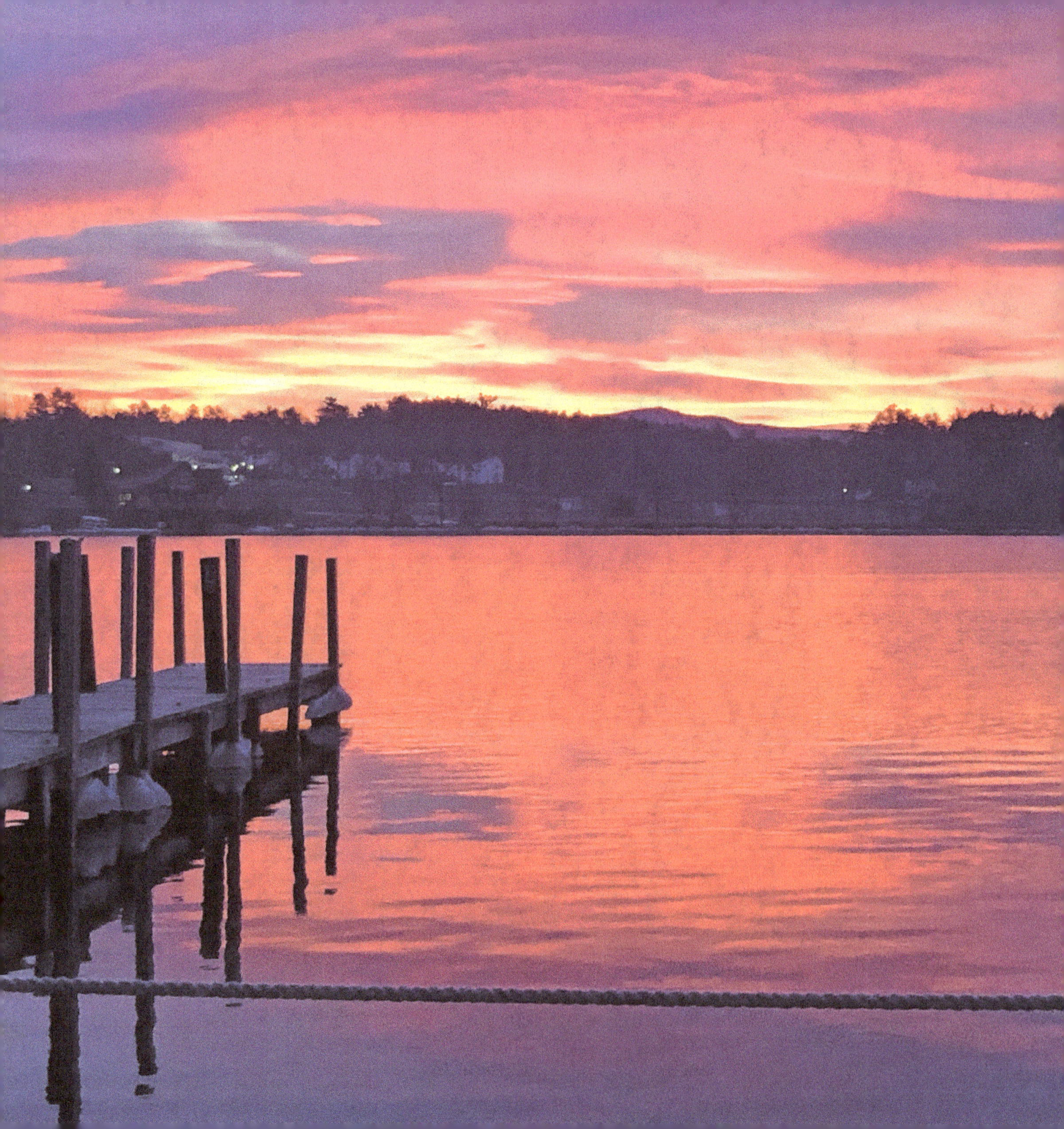

May March's vibrancy
delight you

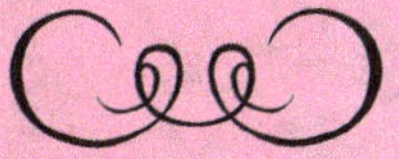

May spring's new
life inspire you today

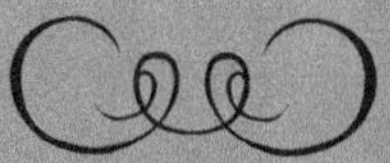

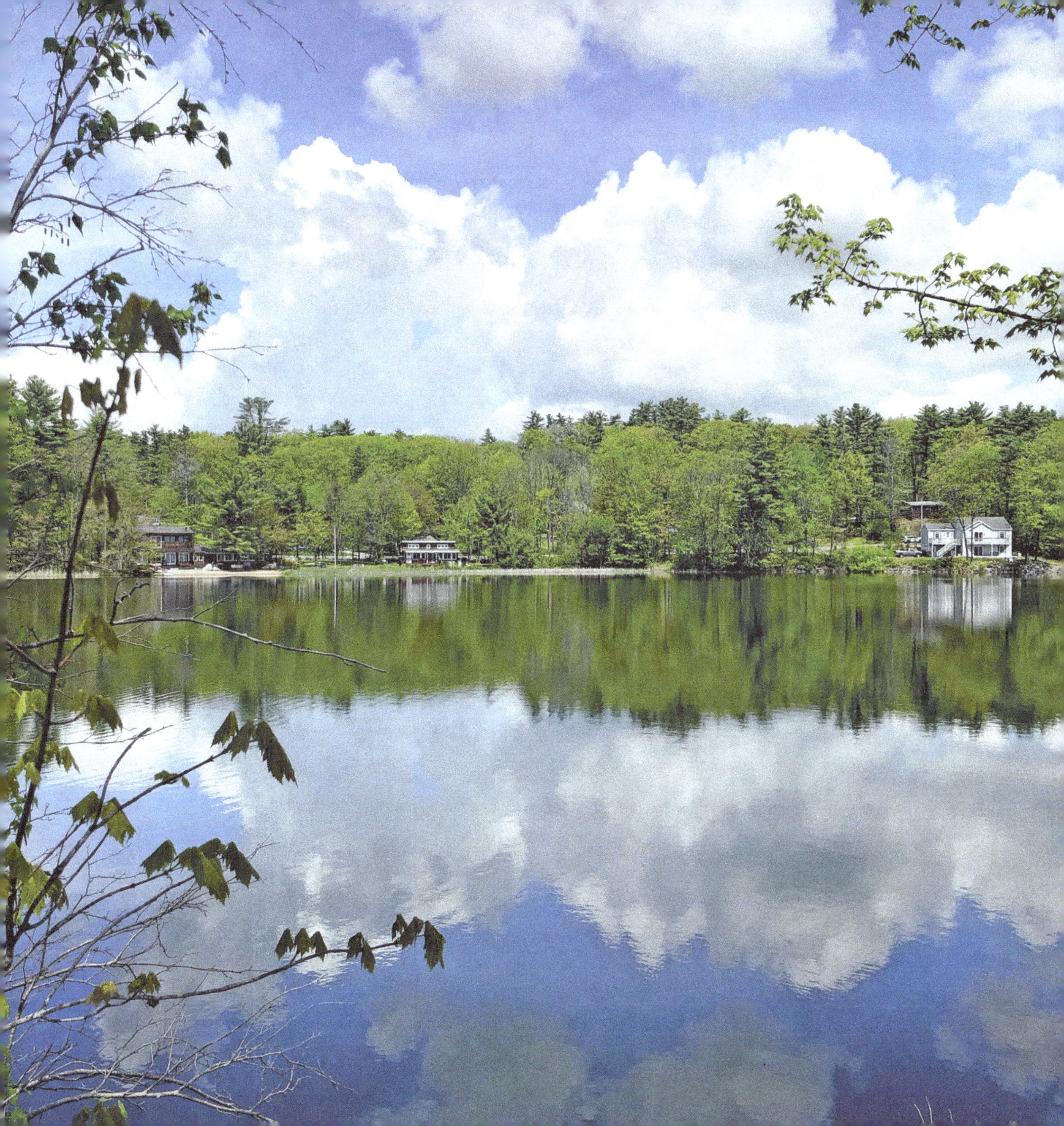

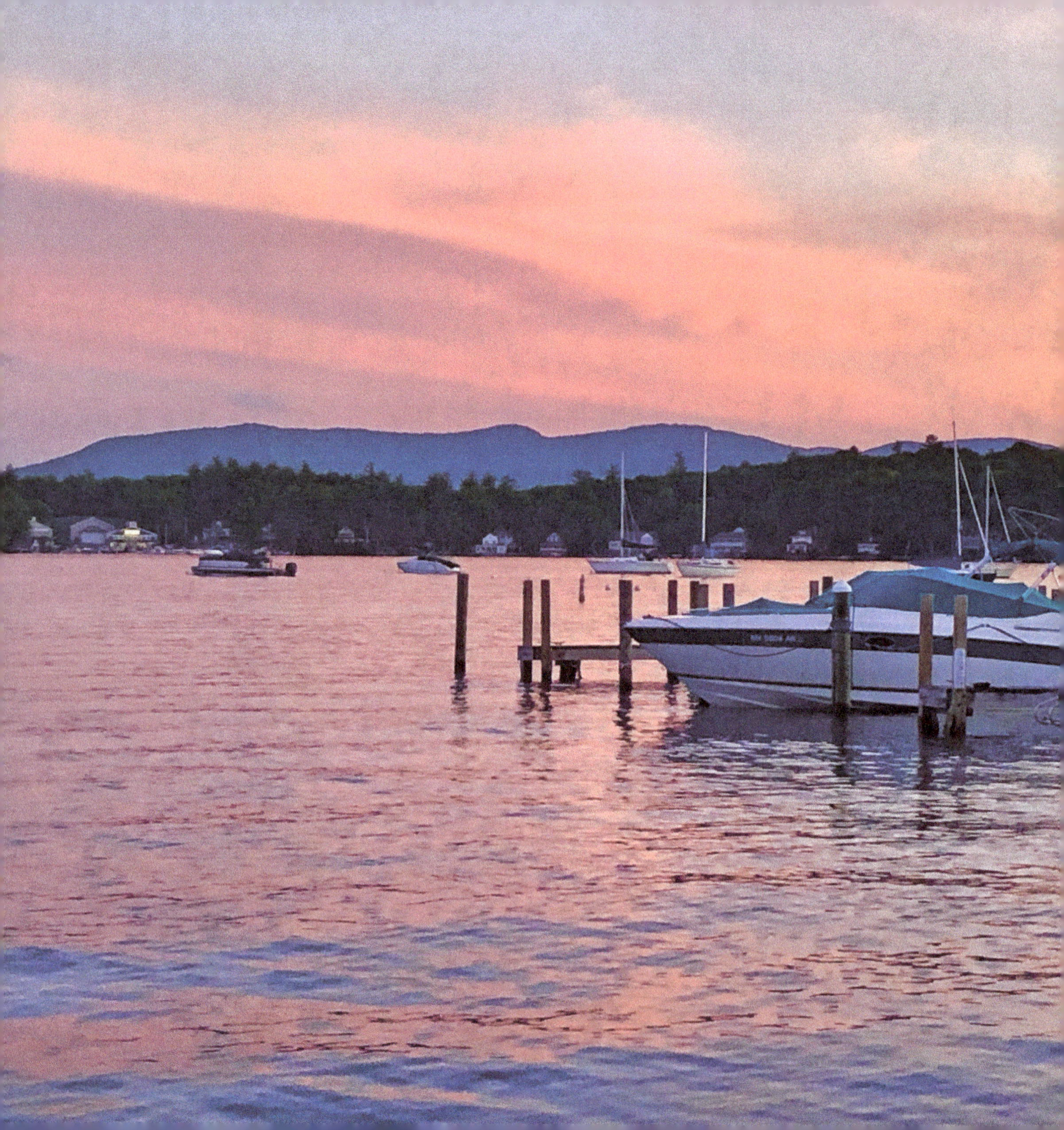

May you breathe
in peace today

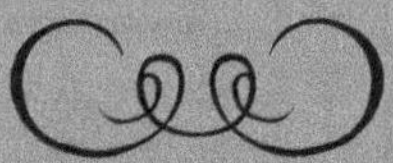

May your day sparkle

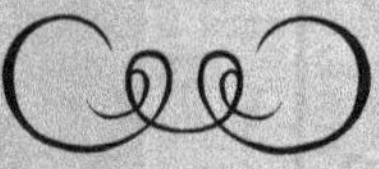

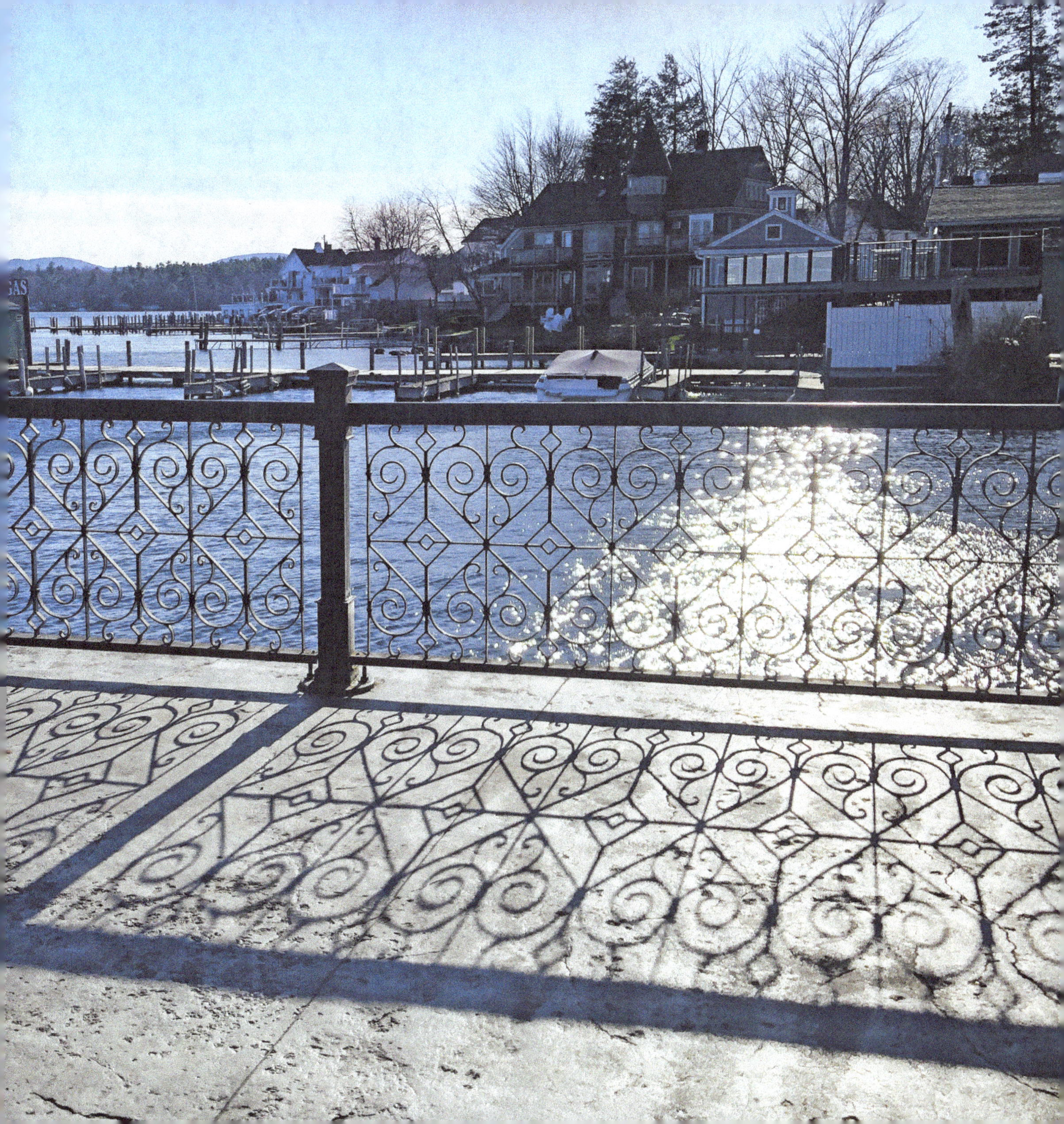

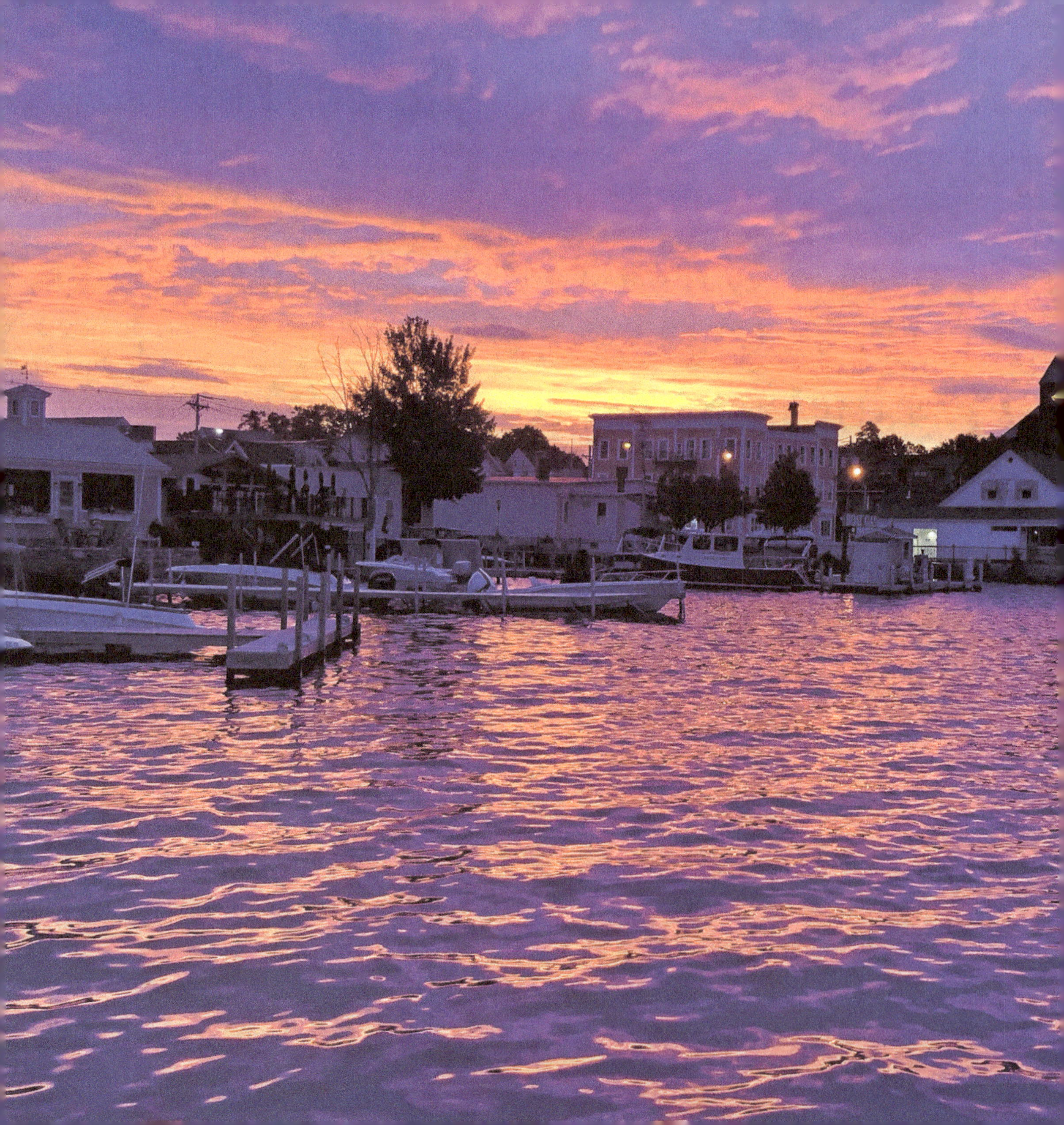

May your kindness
light up the world

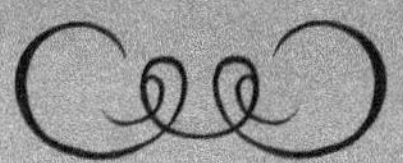

May spring's creativity charm you today

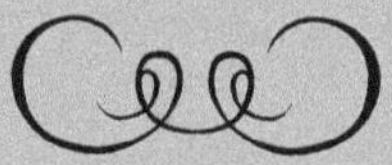

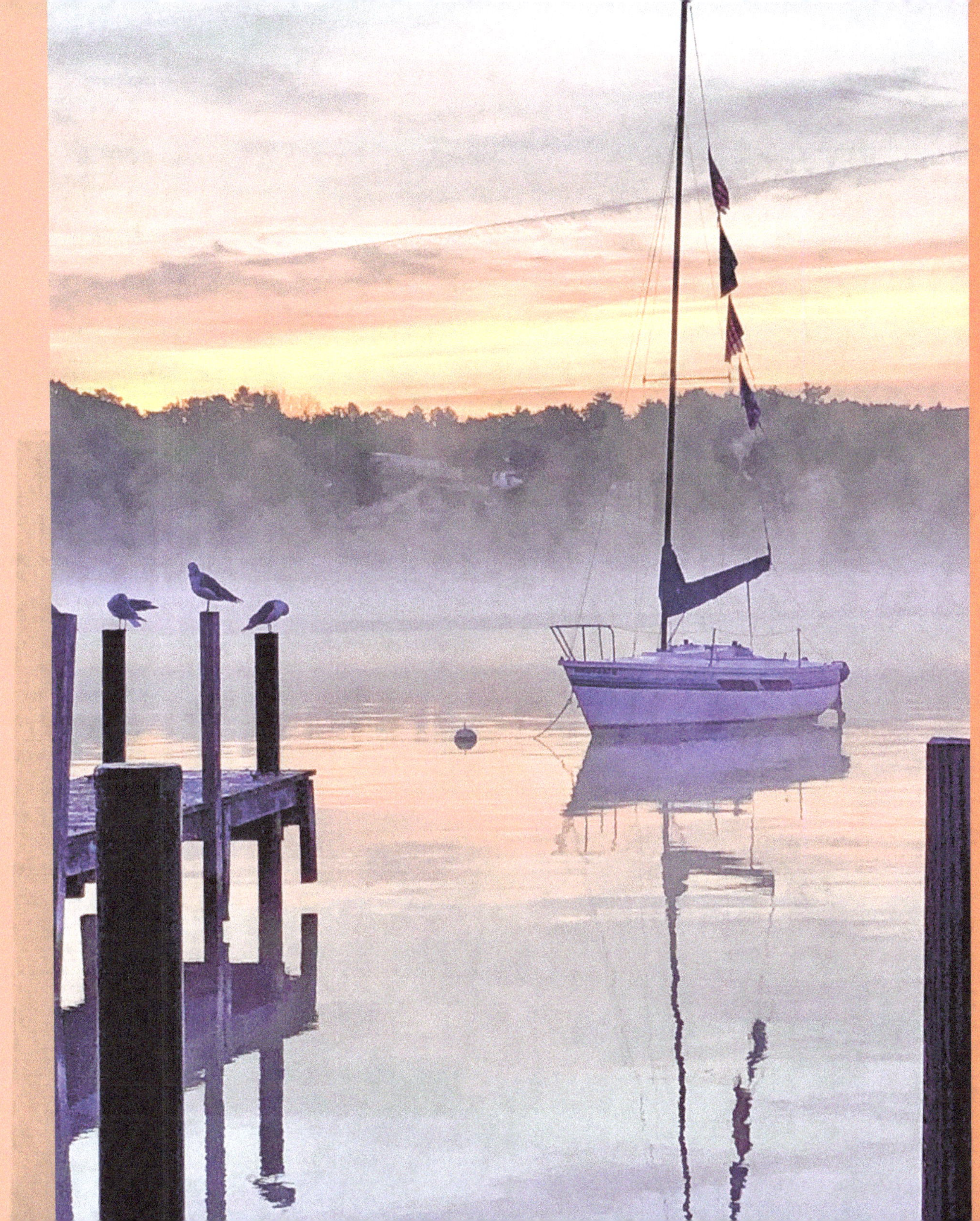

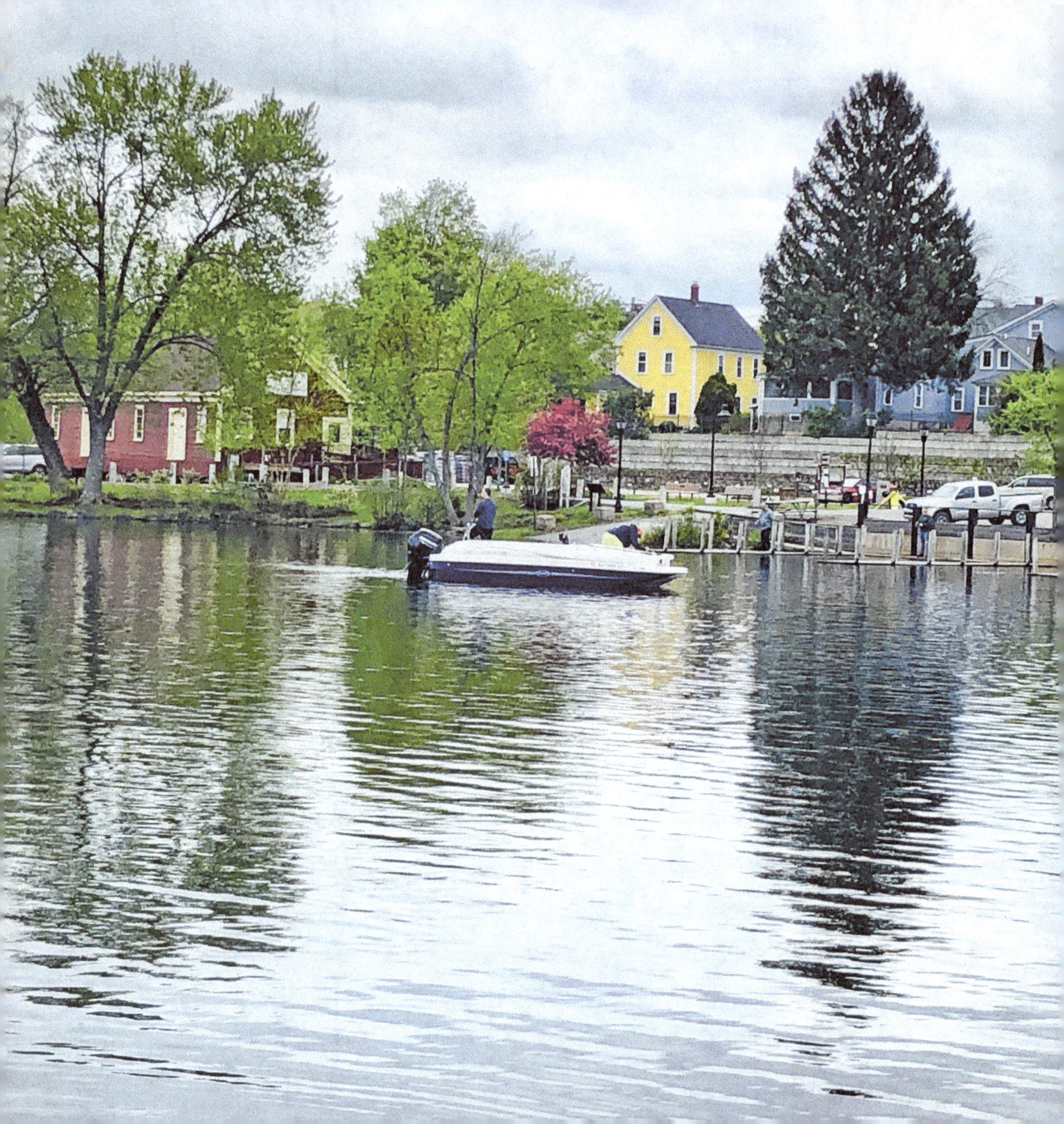

May you find beauty
even on a gray day

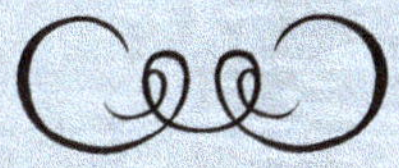

May April's light burst forth to guide you

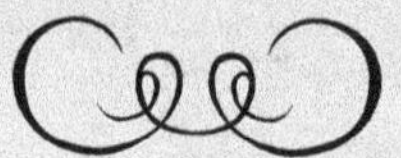

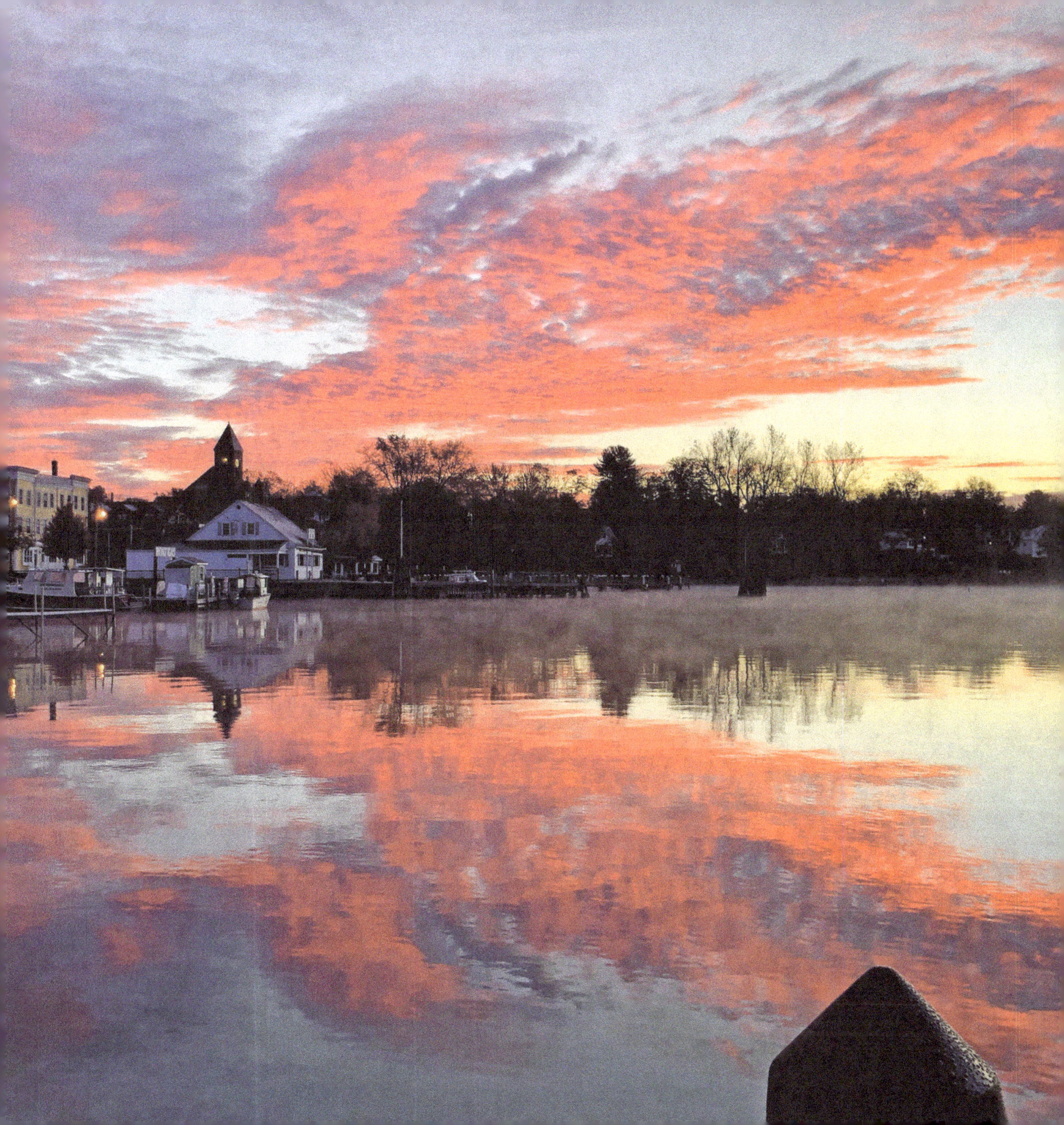

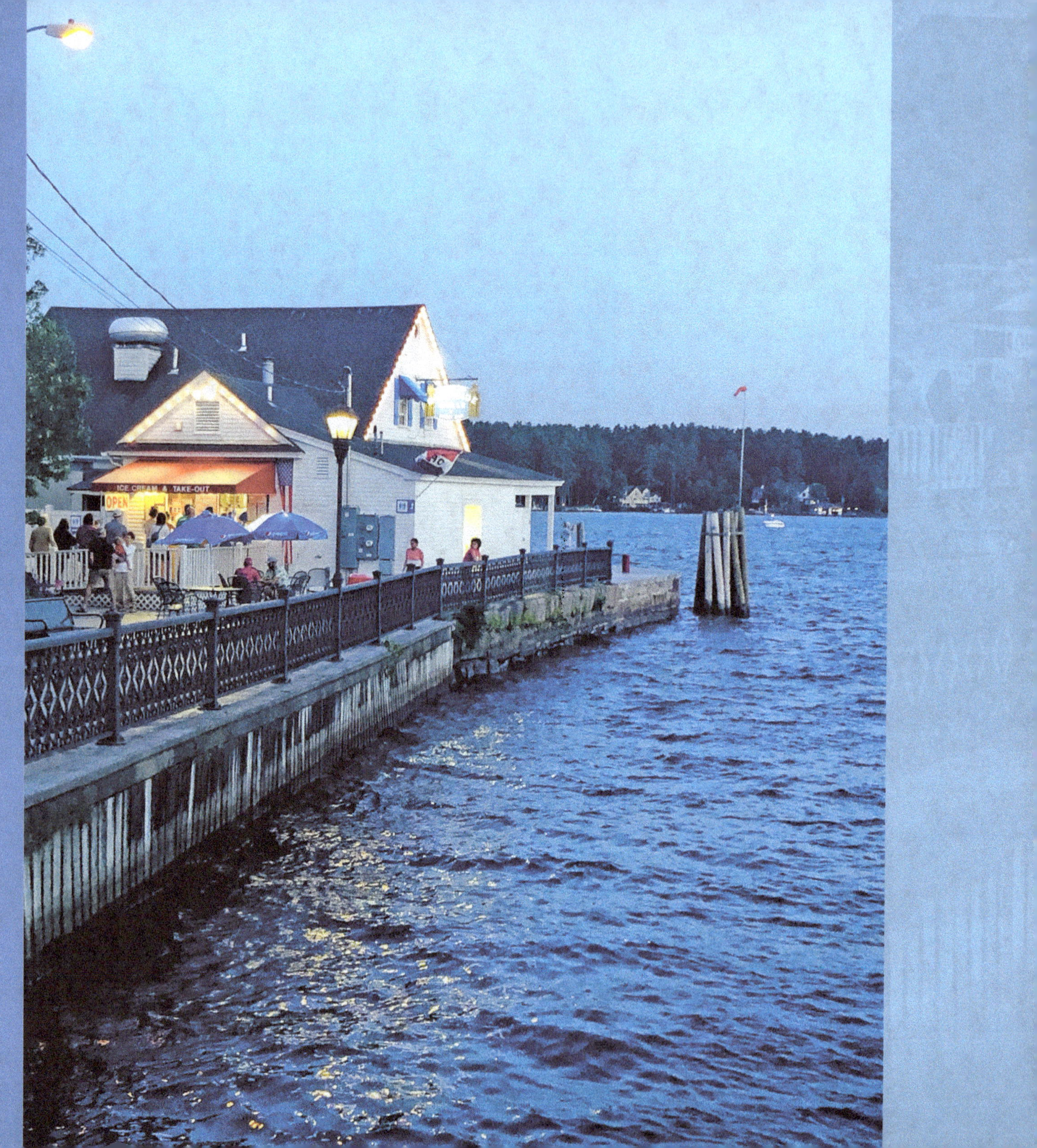

ICE CREAM & TAKE-OUT
OPEN

May you happily remember
the fun of a summer evening

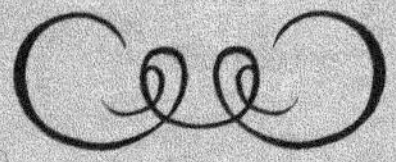

May you fill your body with yummy foods

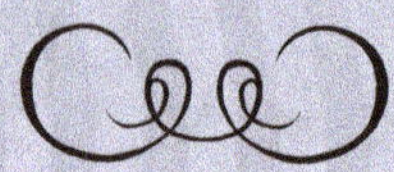

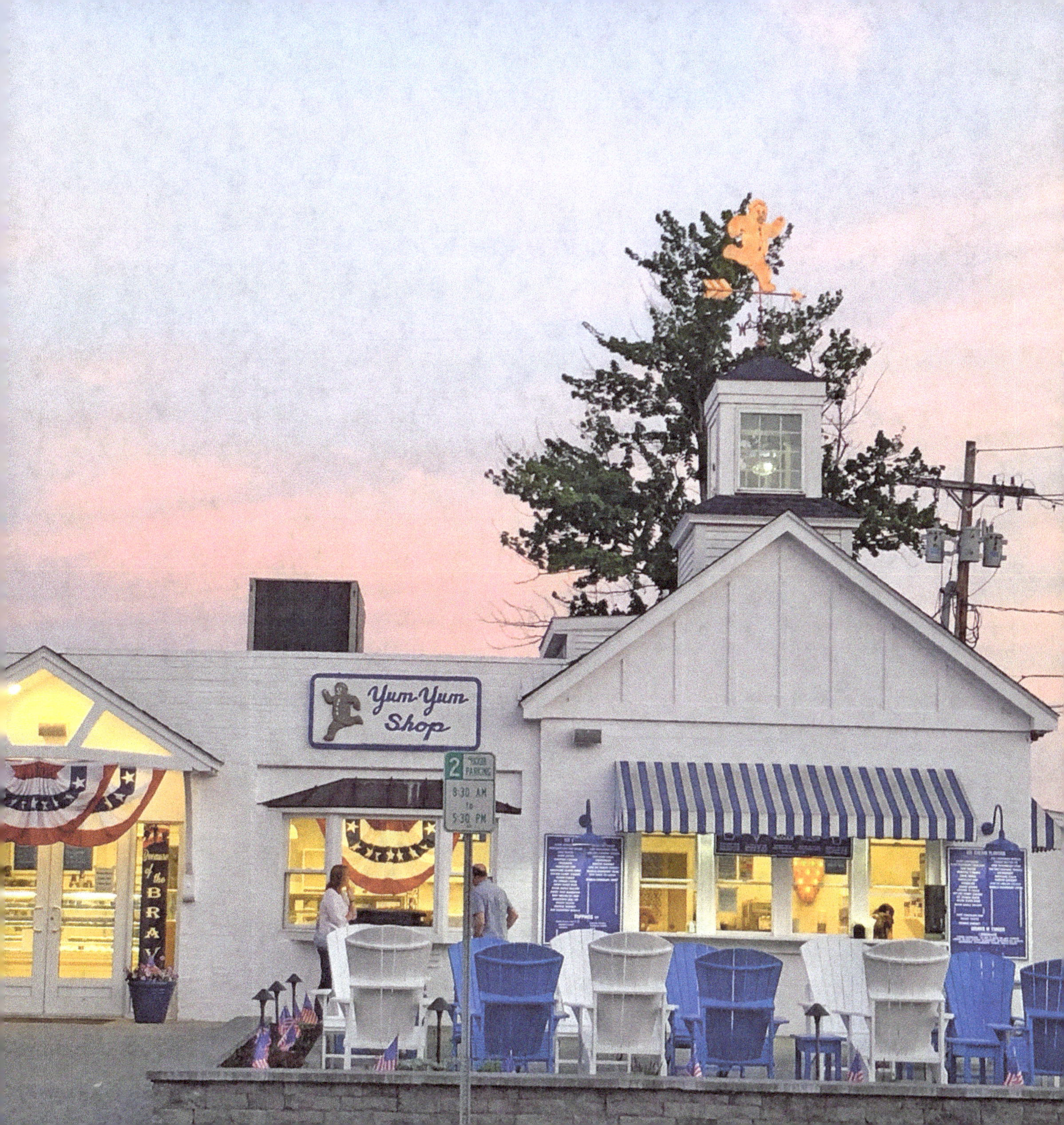

Yum Yum
Shop
2 HOUR PARKING
9:30 AM
to
5:30 PM
BRAV

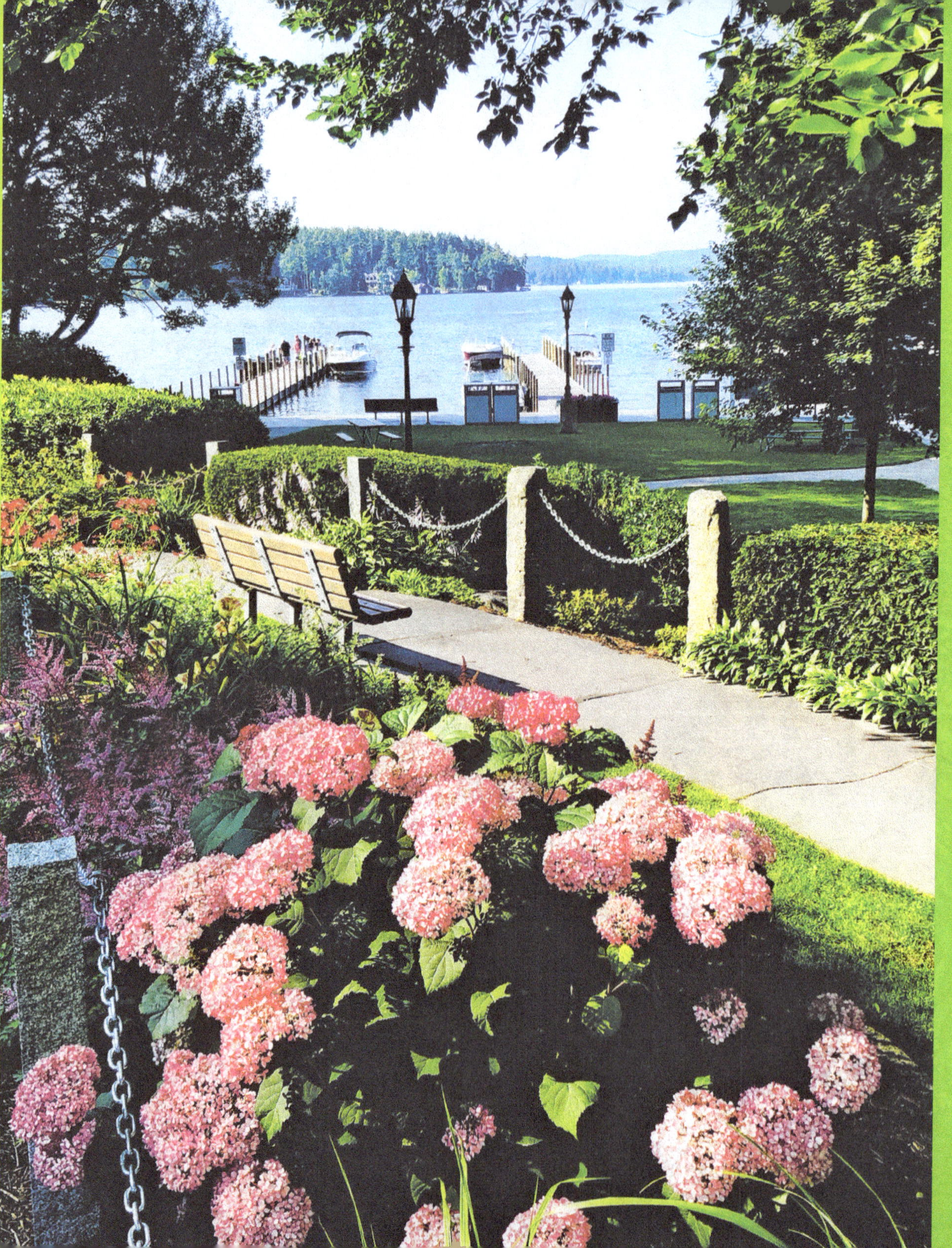

May summer's gardens

rejuvenate you

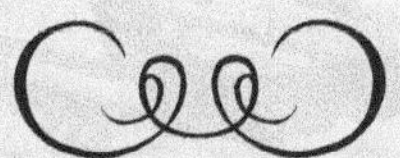

May you find fun
adventures today

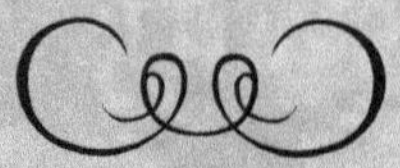

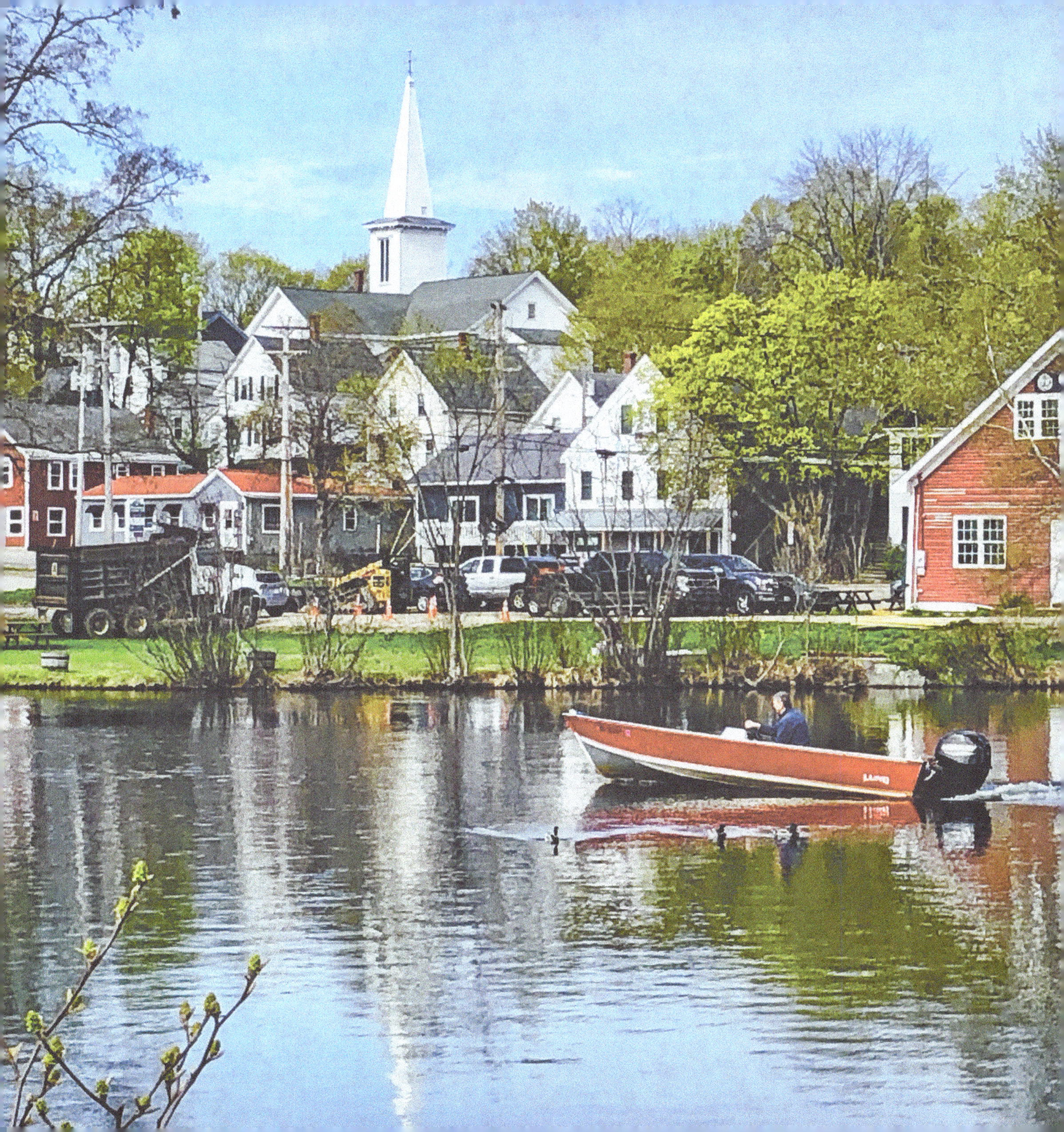

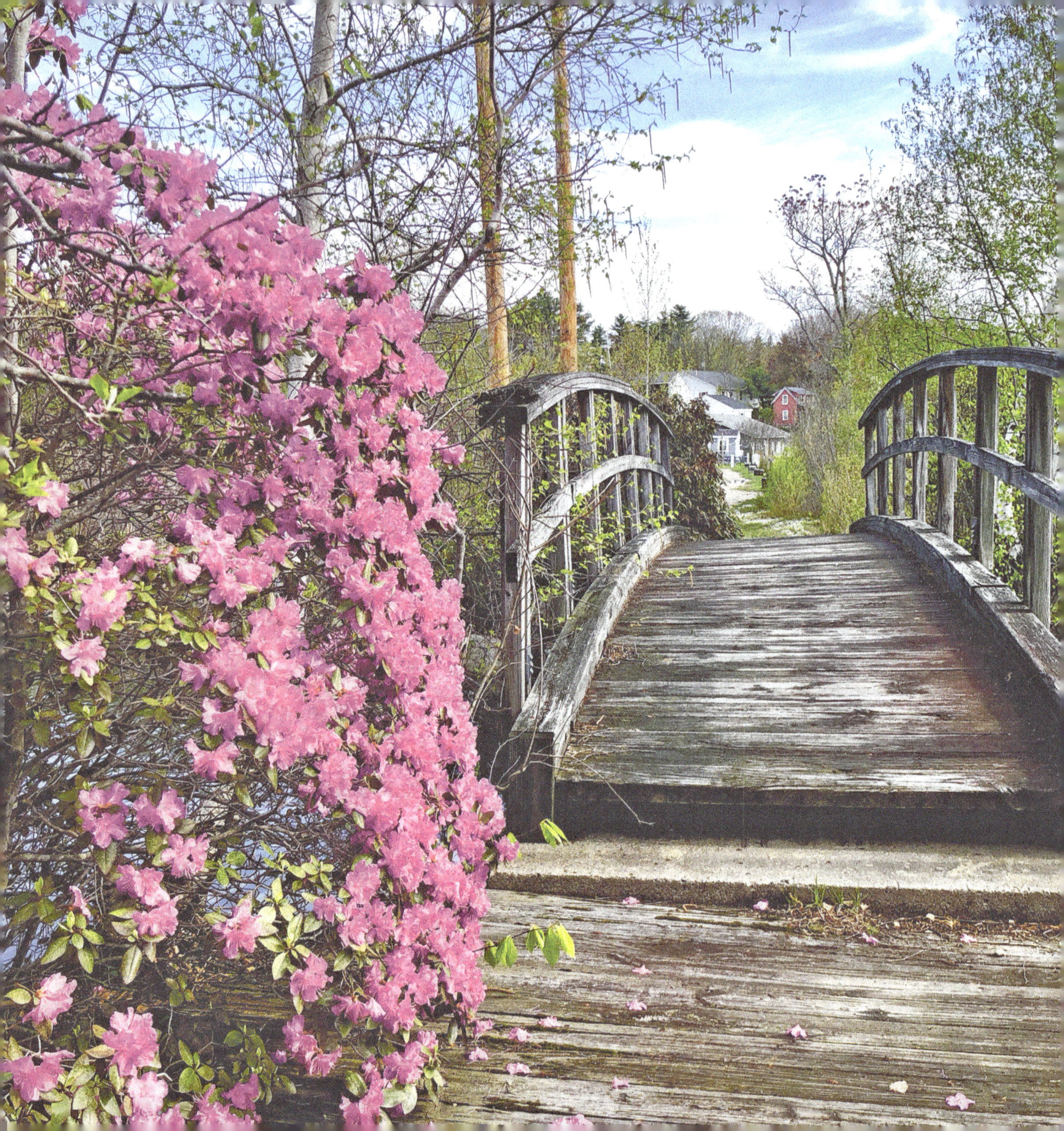

May you delight
in a hidden path

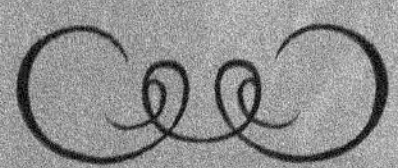

May July's sunset
soothe your soul

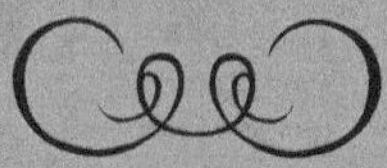

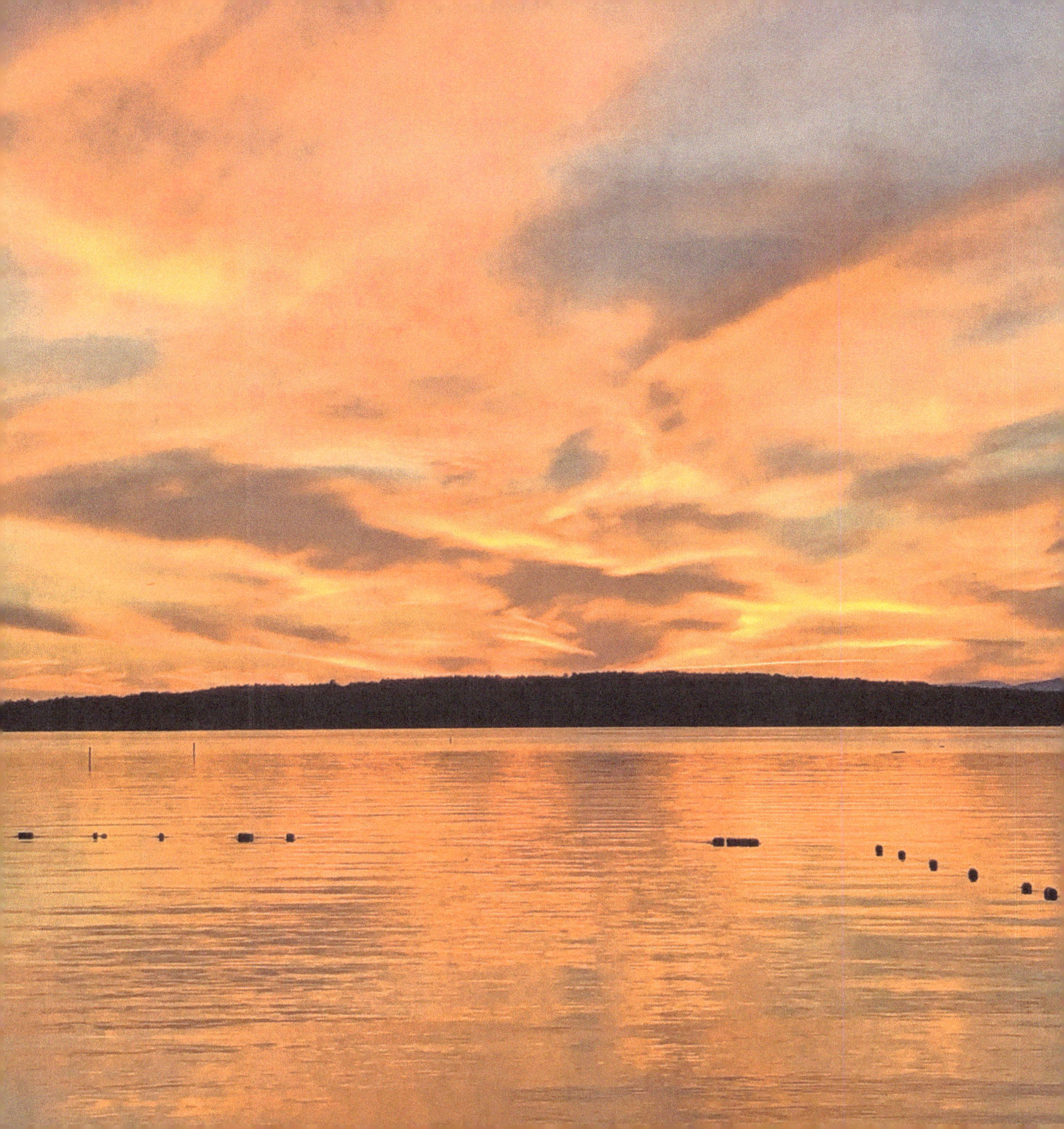

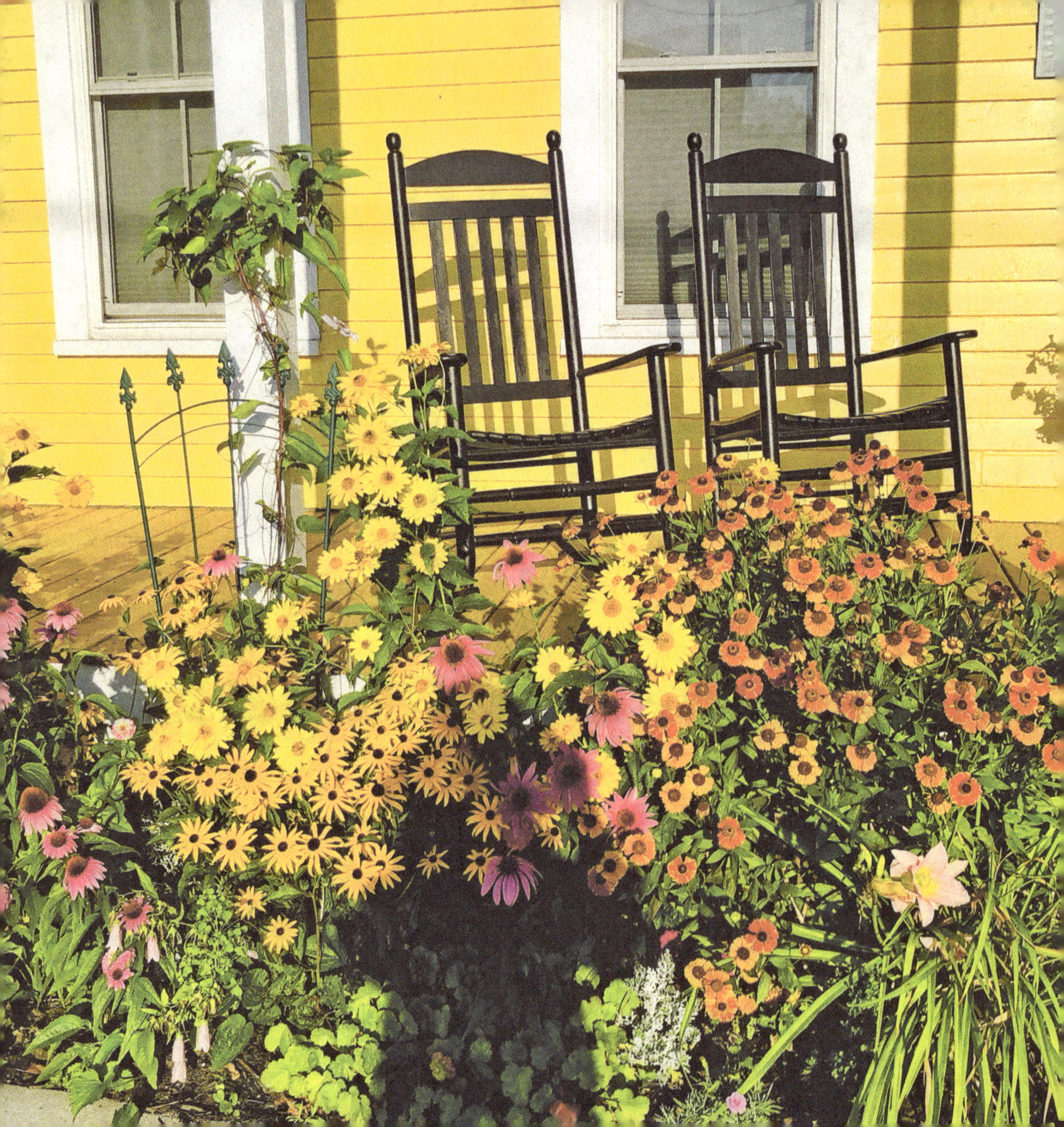

May the blessing of these
flowers fill your heart

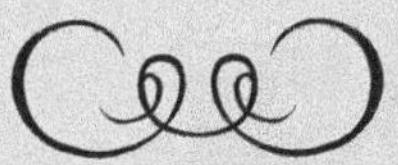

May we celebrate our freedom with gusto

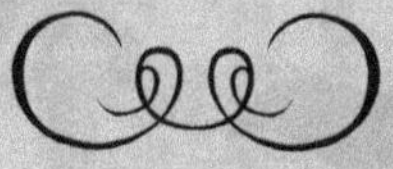

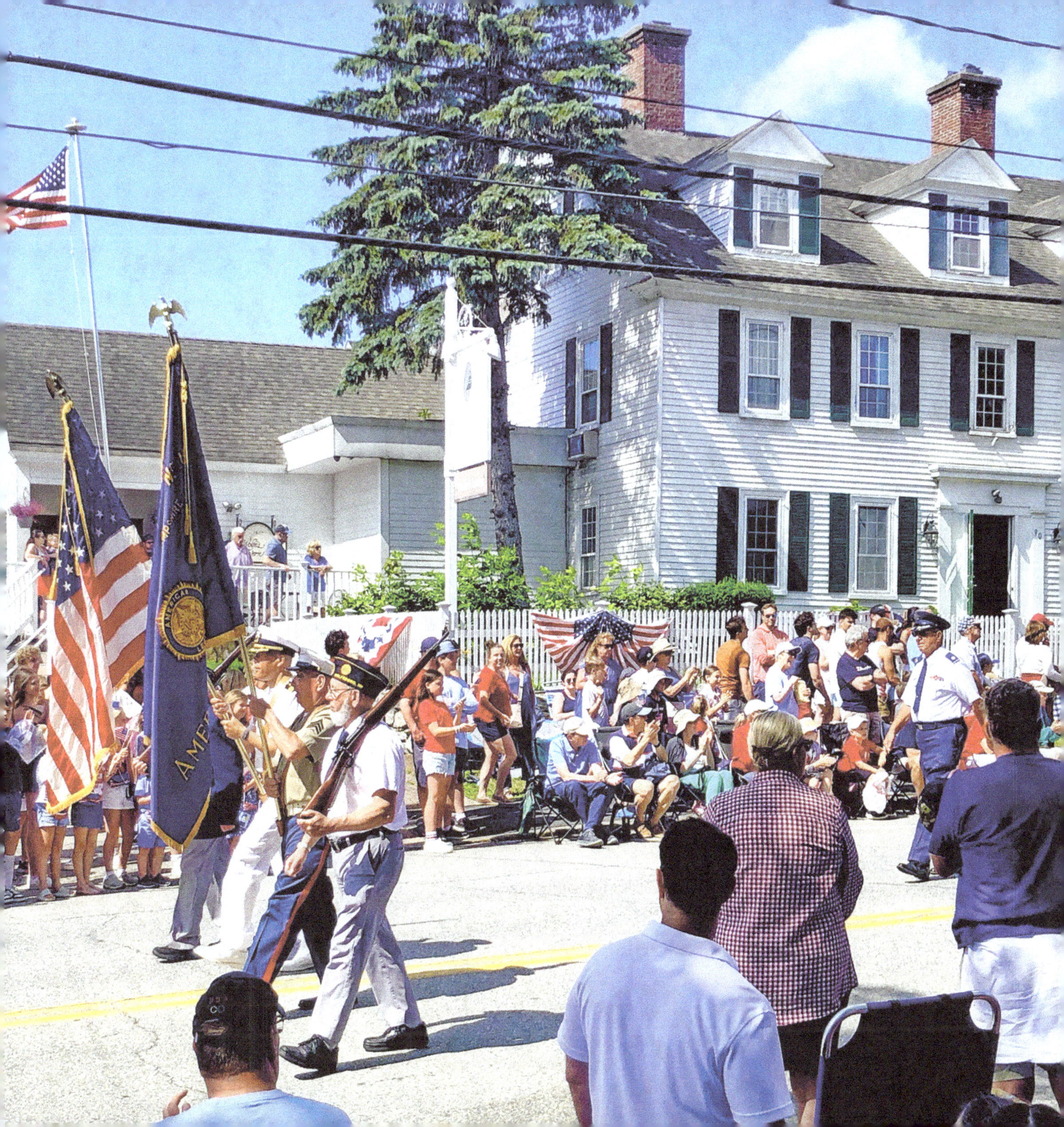

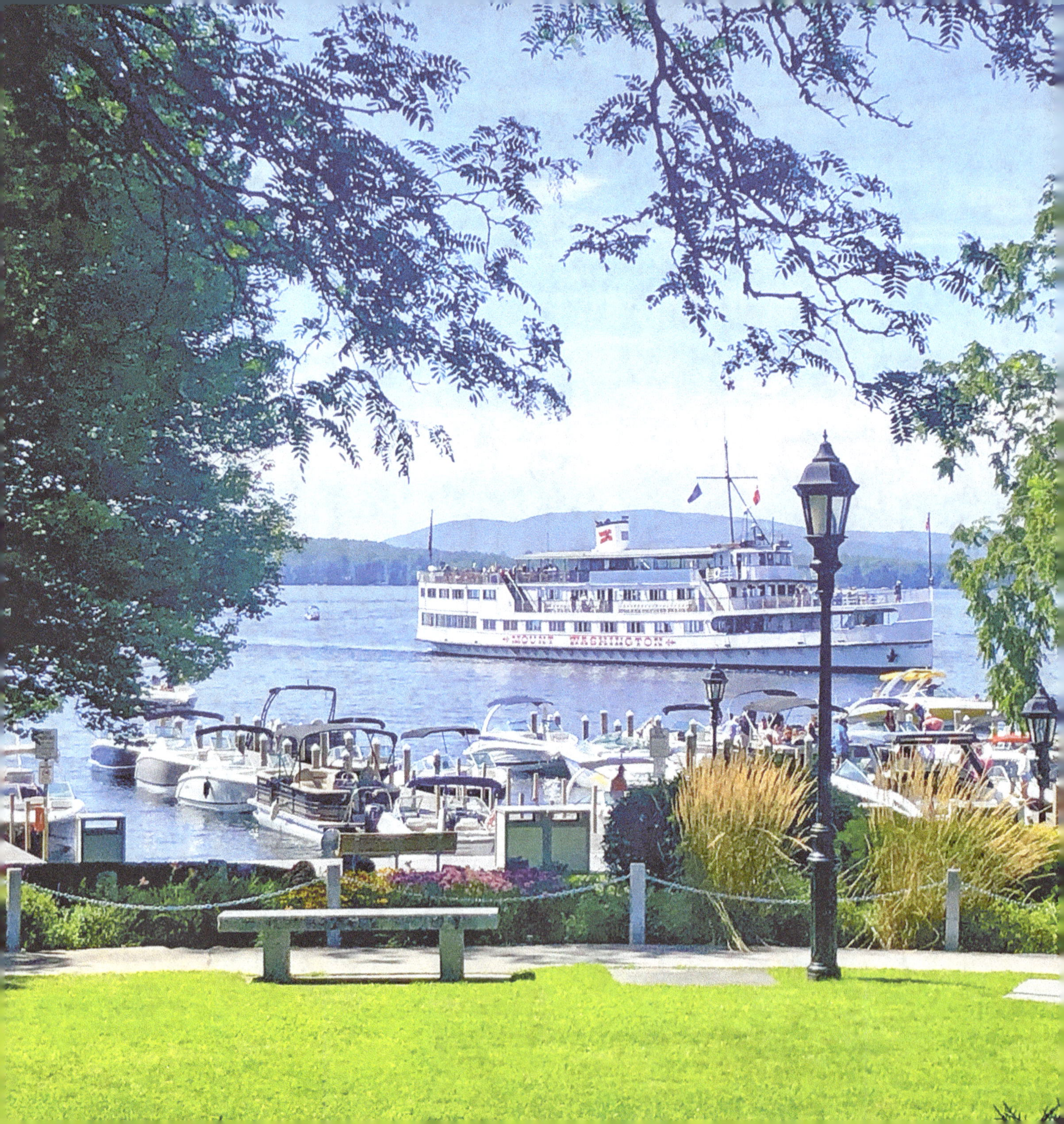

MOUNT WASHINGTON

May you enjoy a fun excursion today

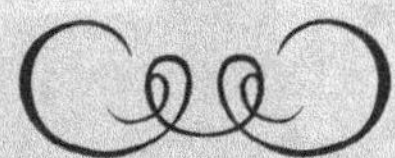

May you relish the beauty of this day

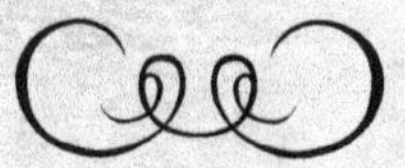

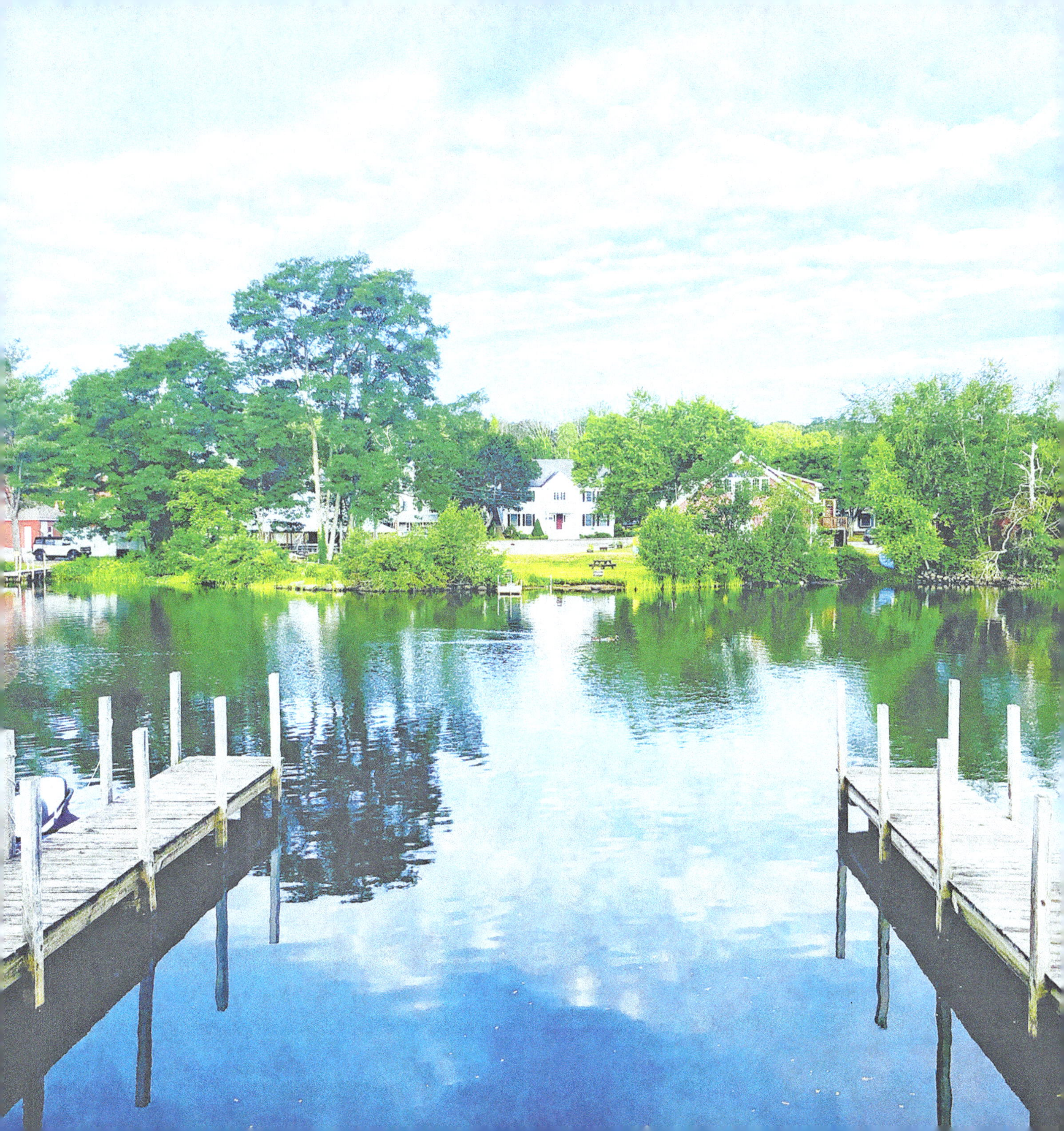

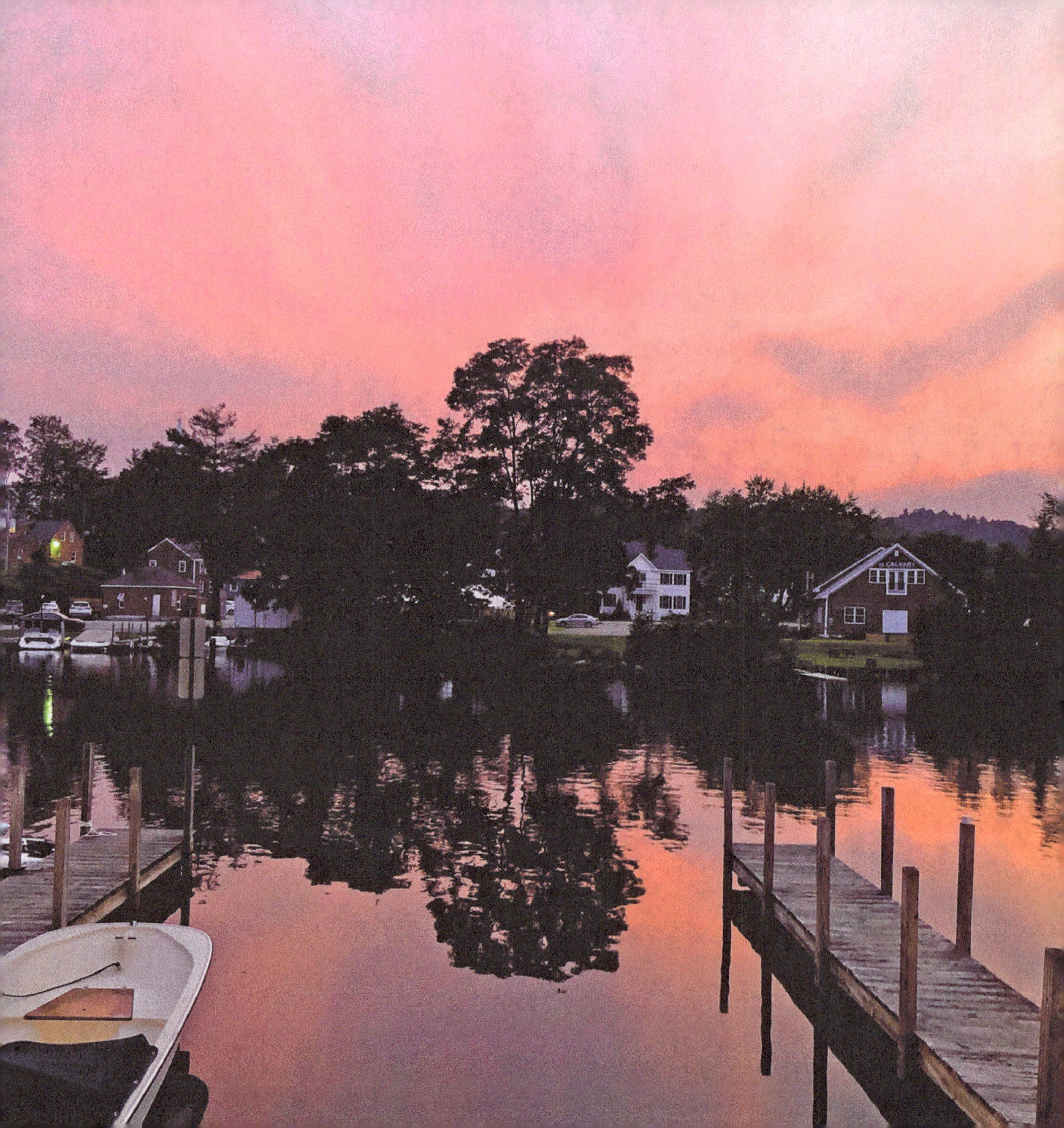

CALVARY

May August's peace
envelop you each day

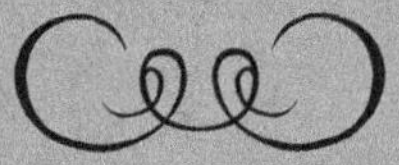

May you stand in awe
of the beauty around you

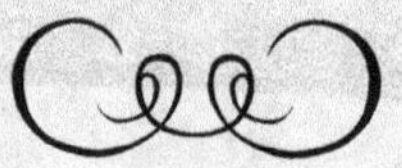

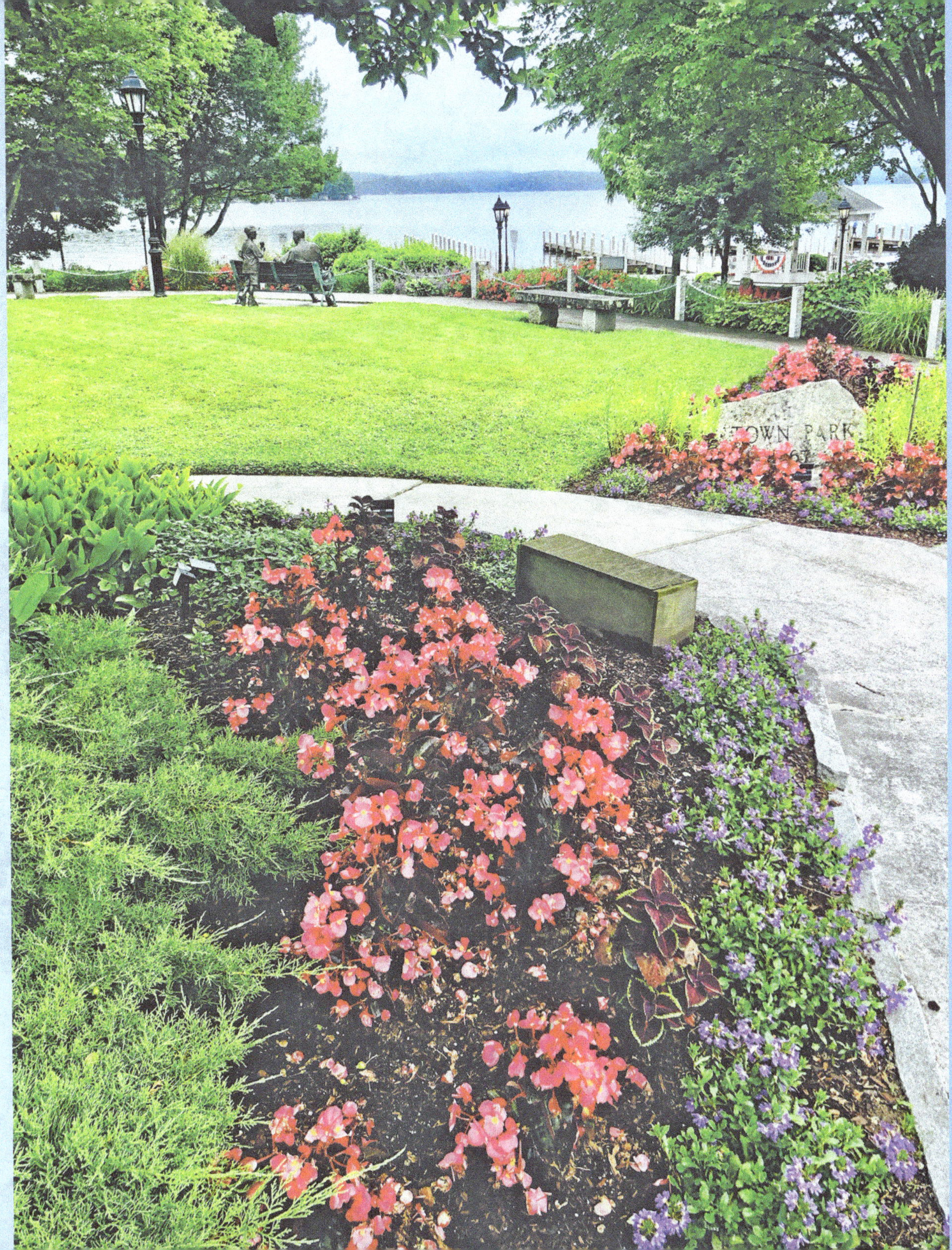

TOWN PARK

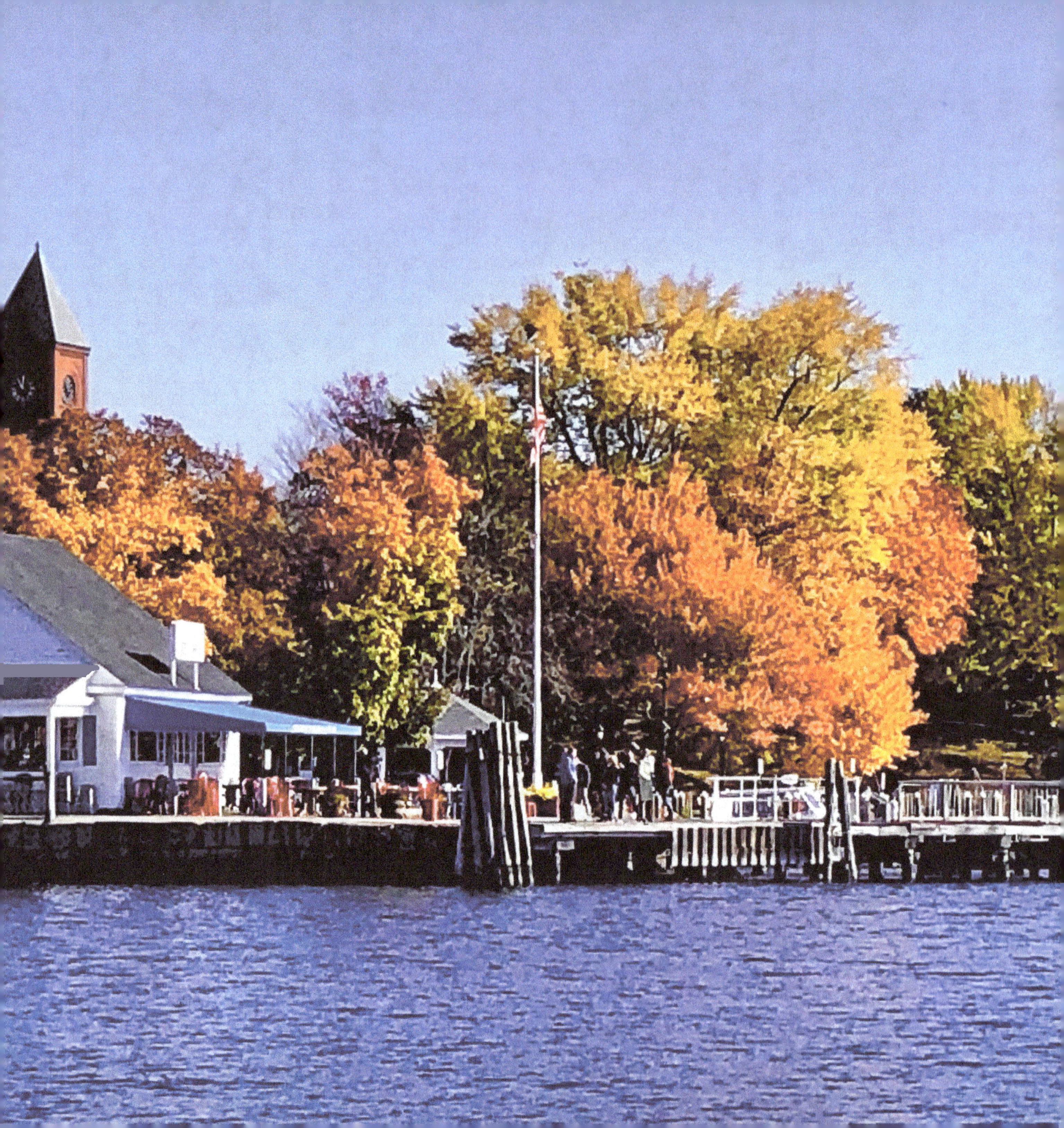

May autumn's colors

uplift you today

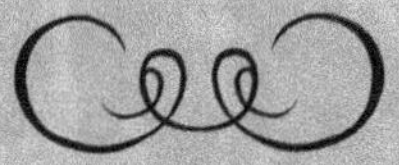

May you breathe in
September's freshness

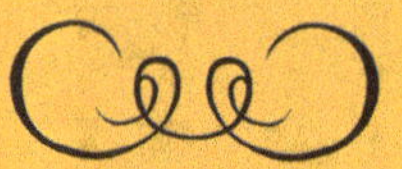

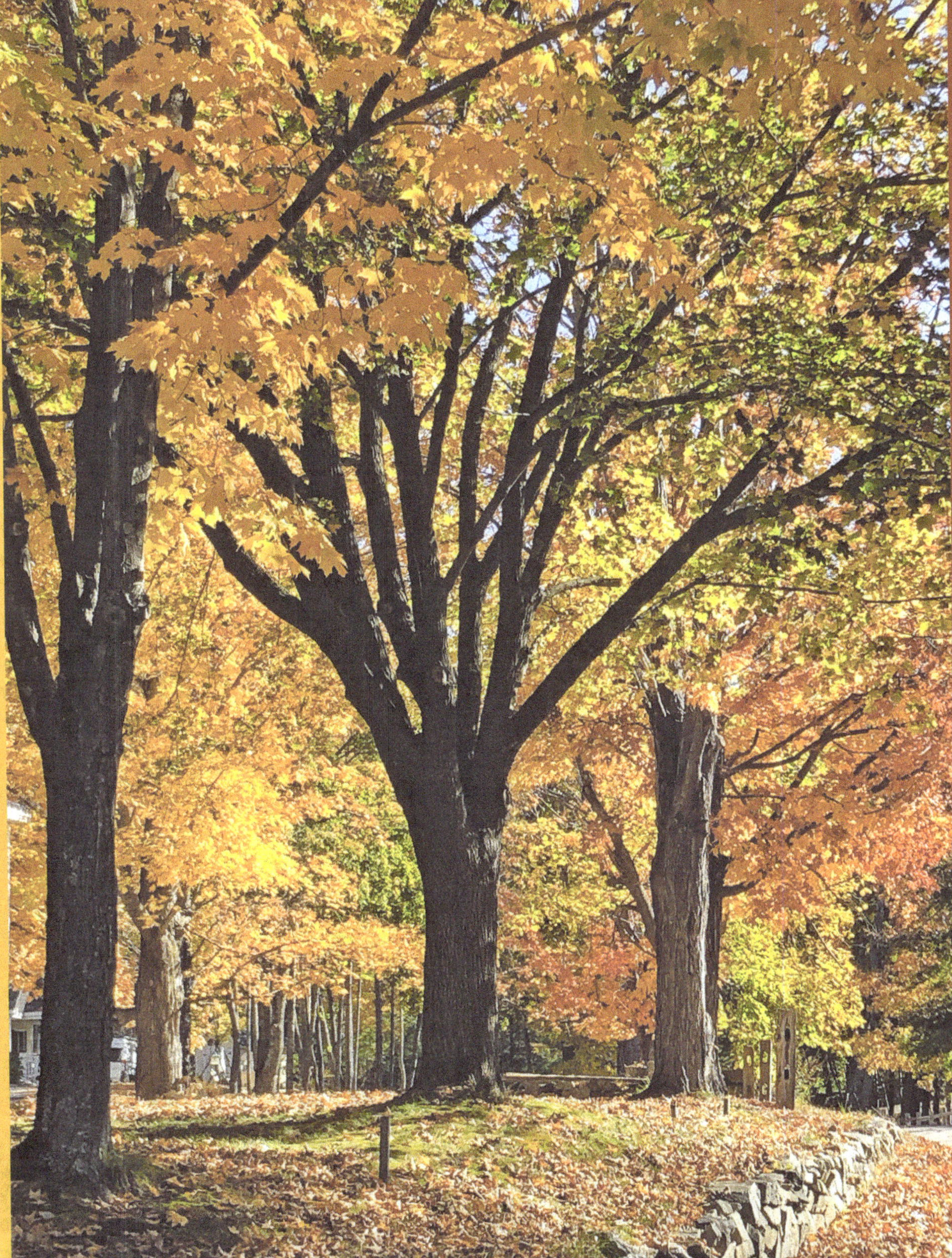

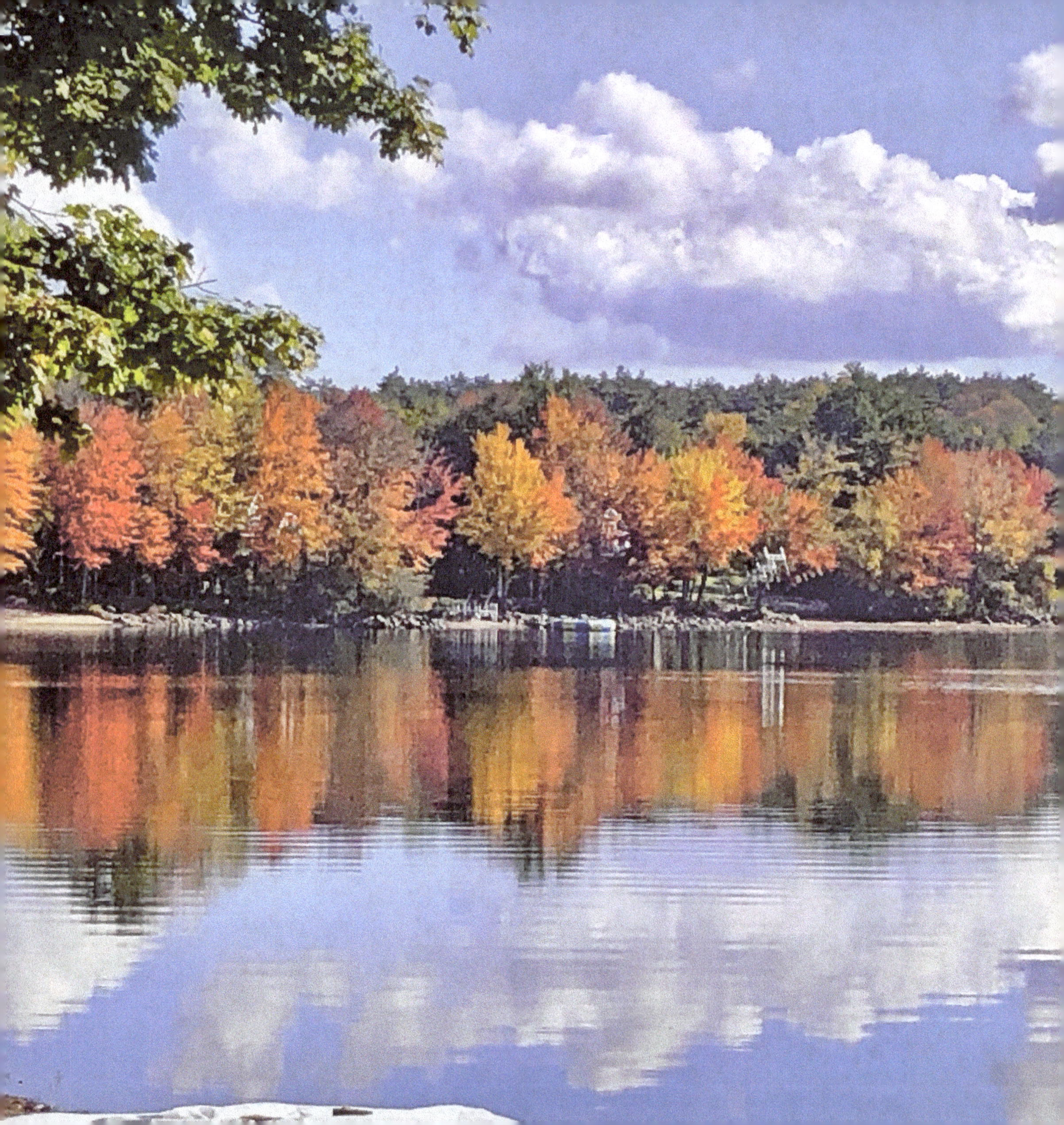

May fall's brilliant colors
wrap you in gladness

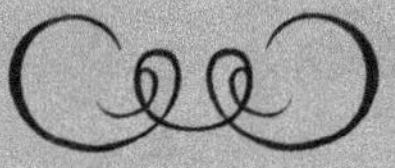

May each day
bring you blessings

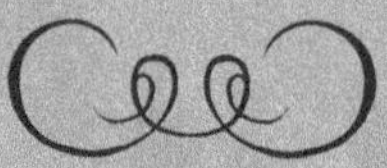

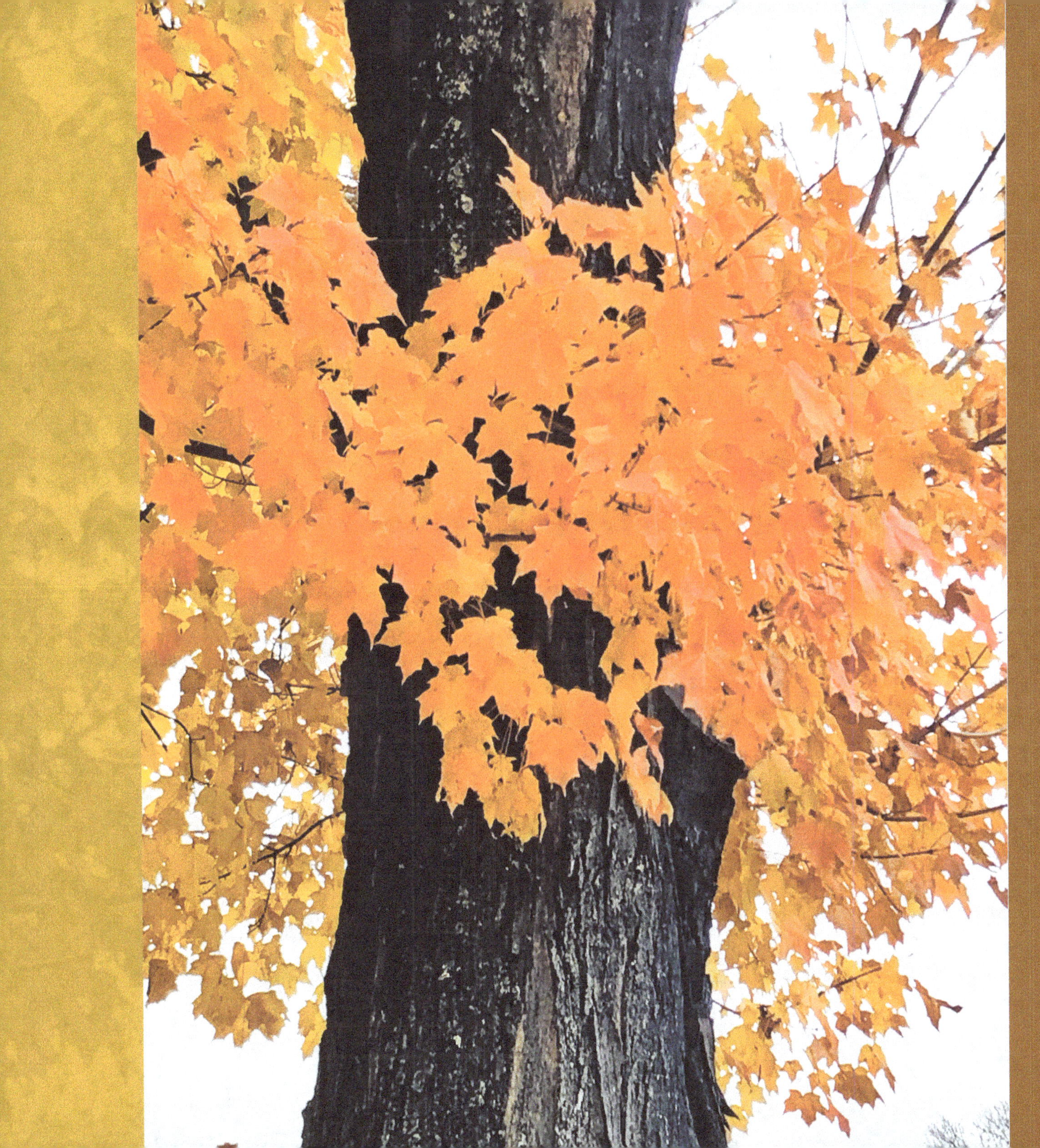

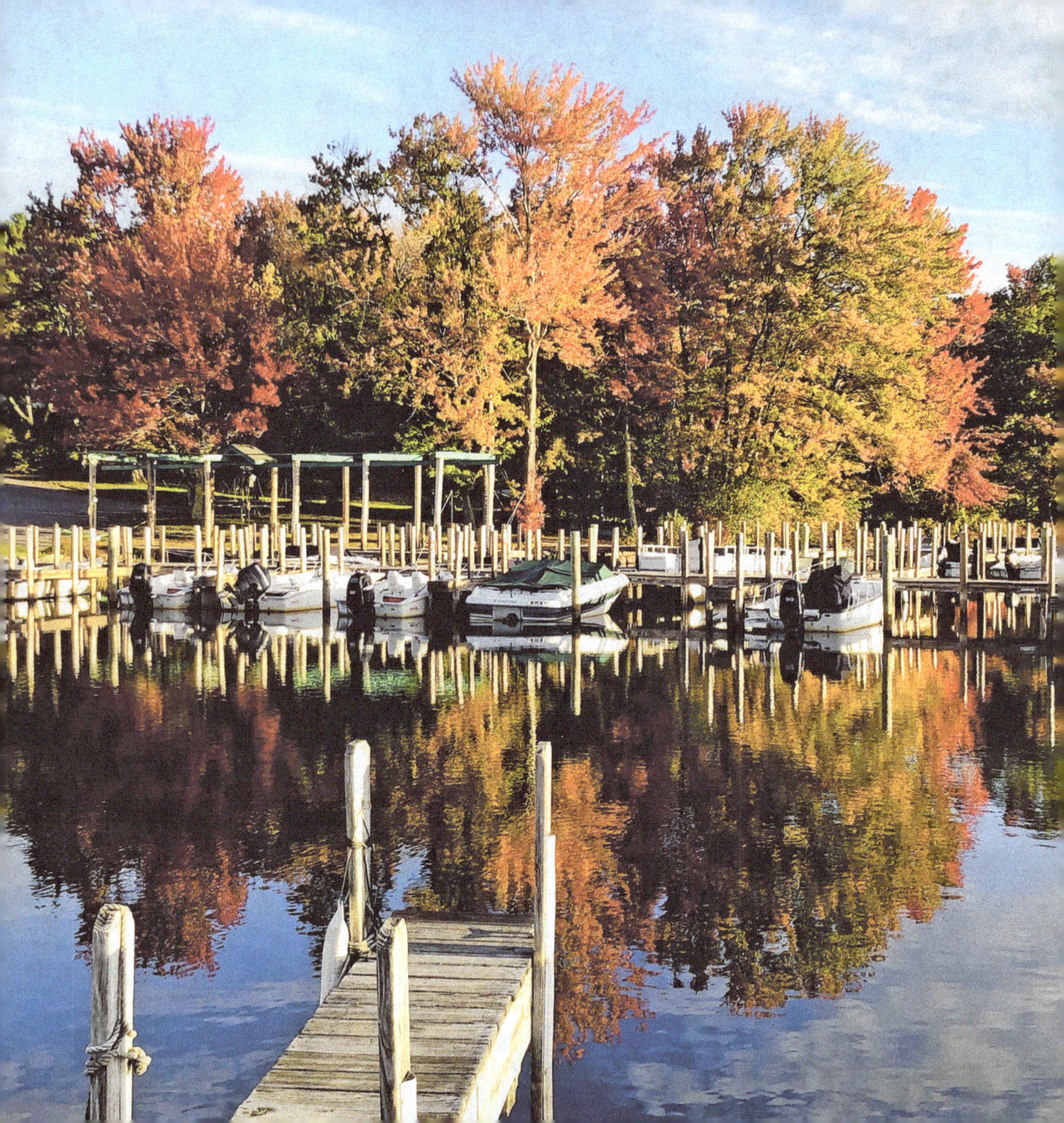

May you feel enheartened
by fall's vibrancy

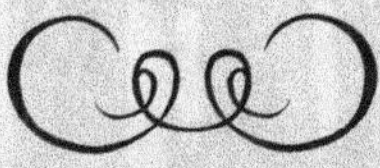

May peace light up your world

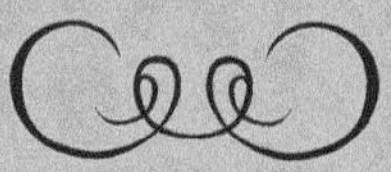

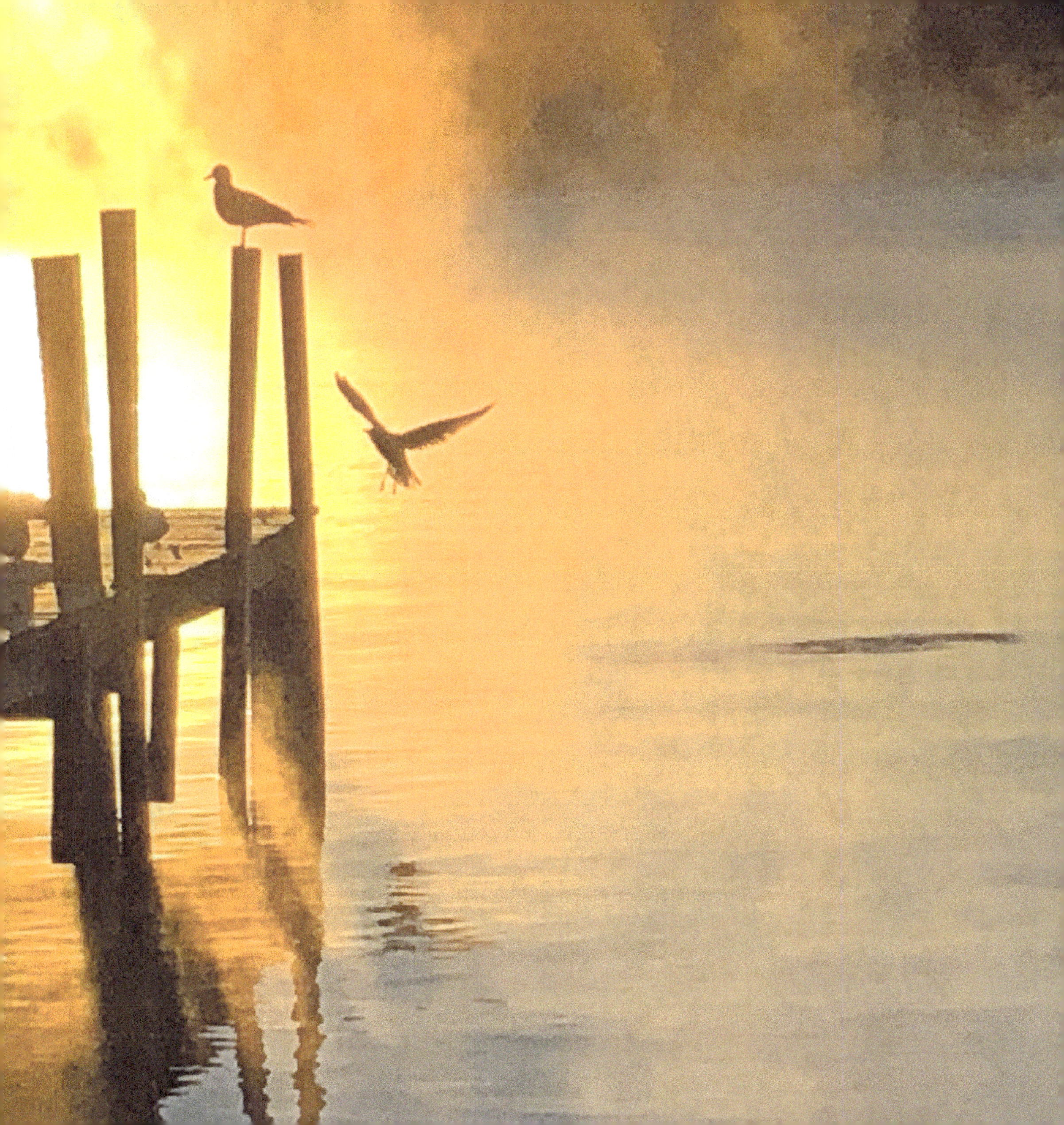

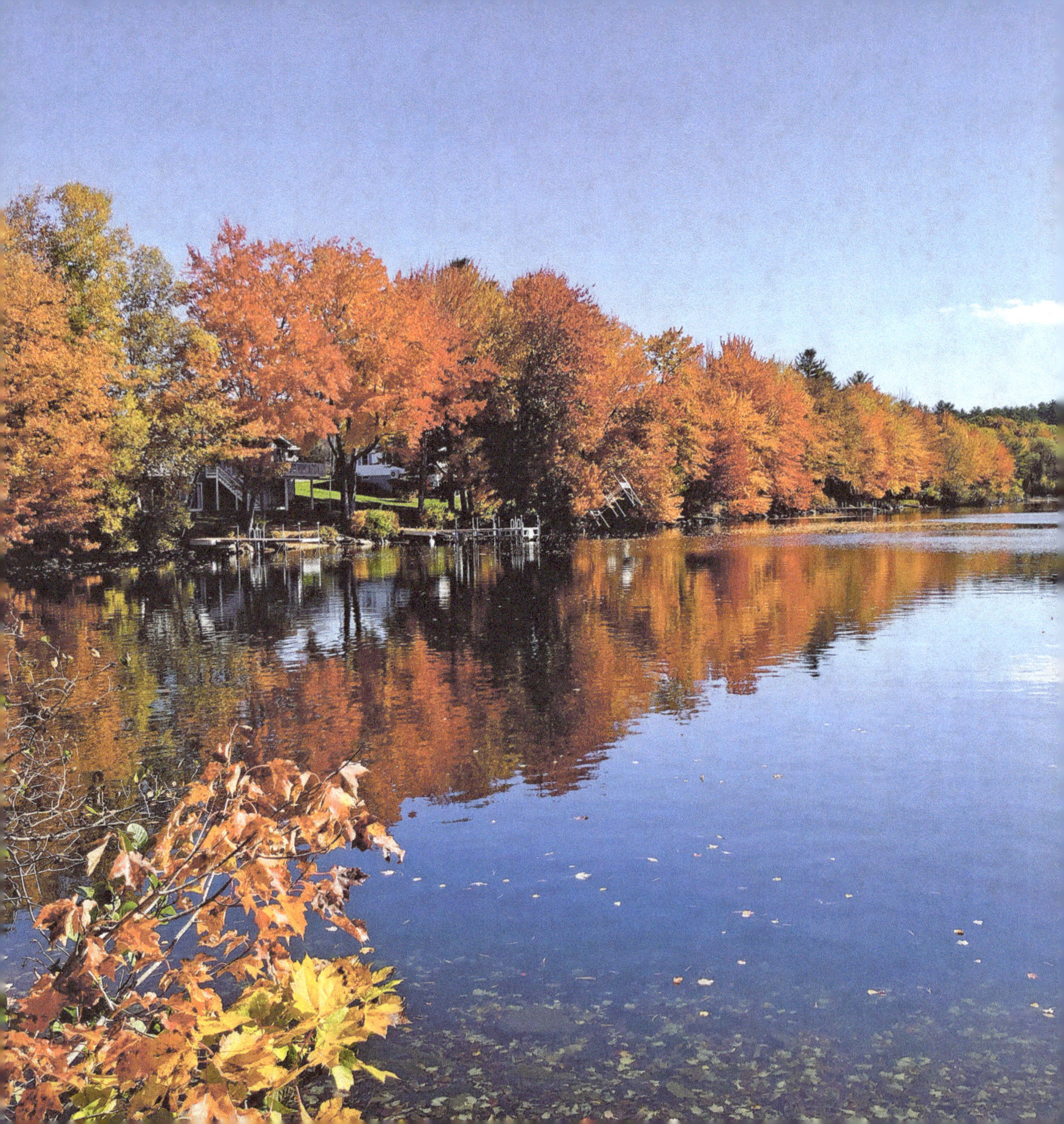

May October's light
warm your spirit

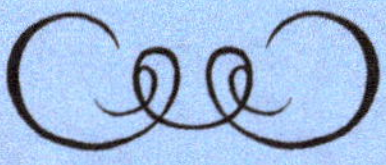

May nature's gifts brighten your day

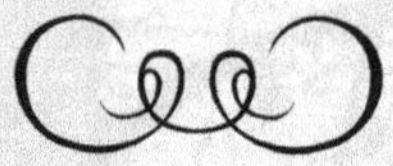

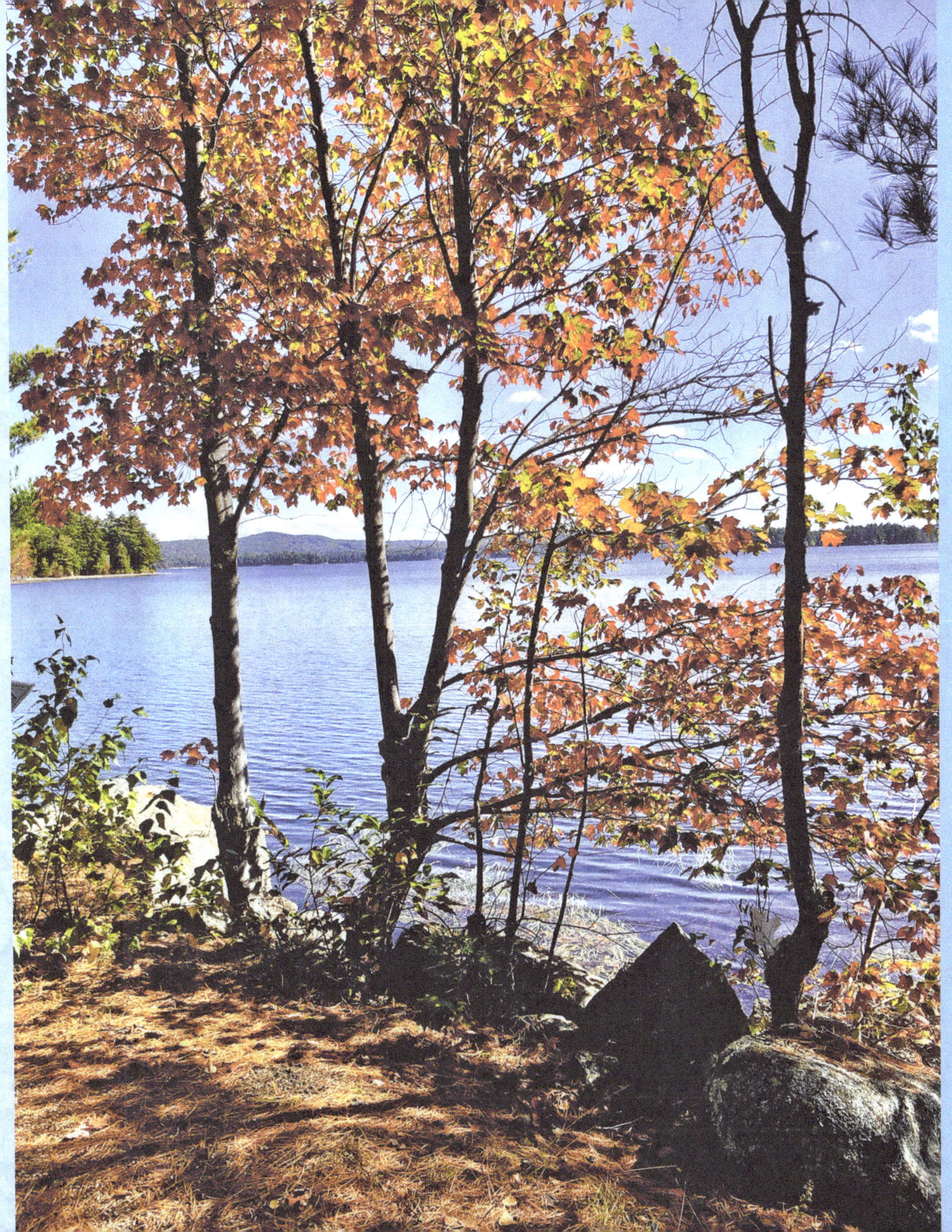

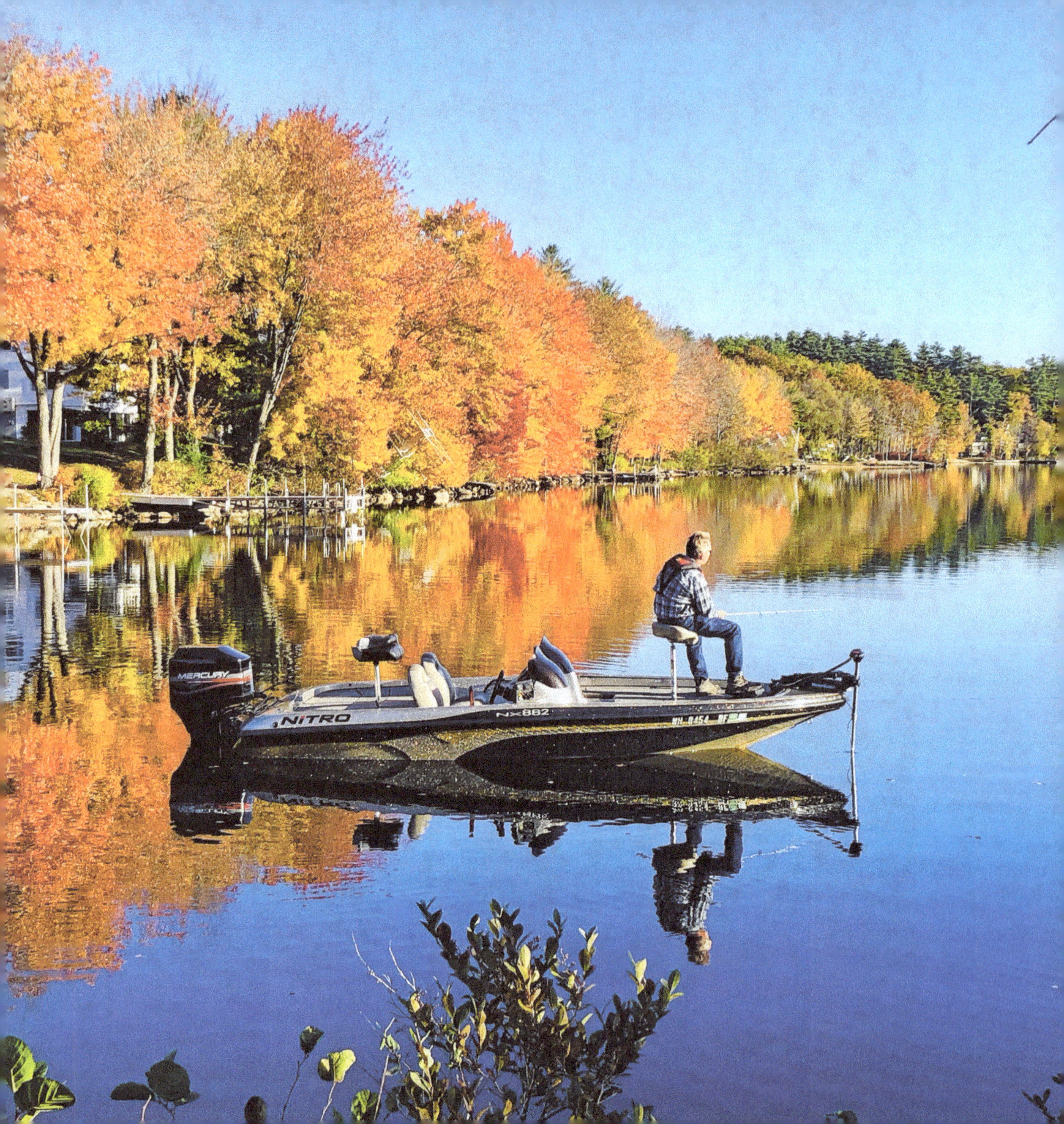

May you embrace this
day with a joyful spirit

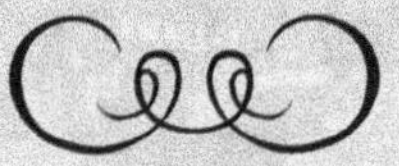

May the softness of
this sunset soothe you

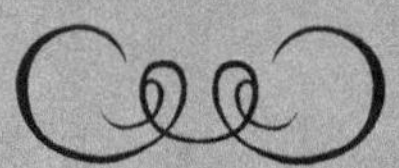

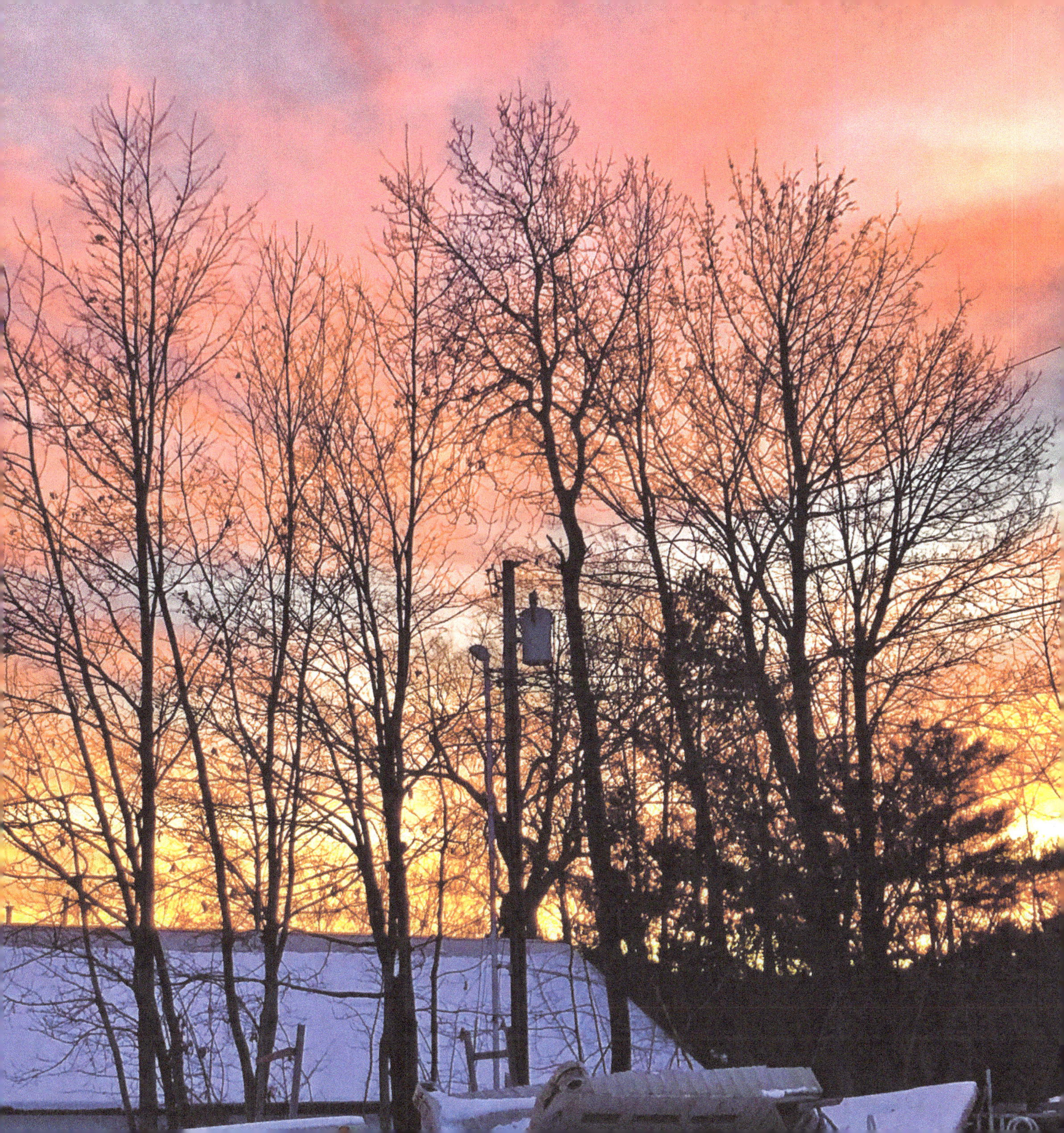

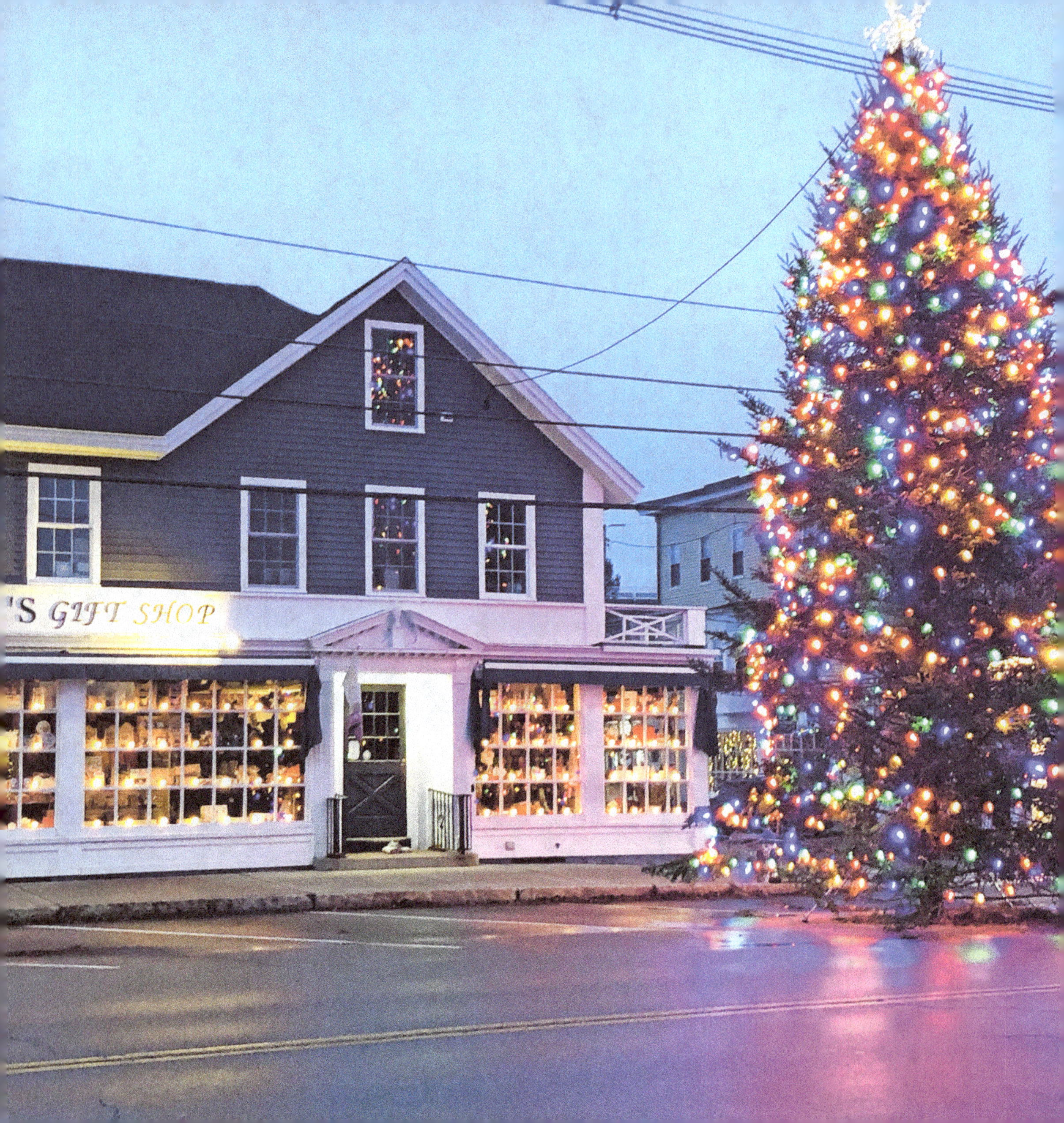
'S GIFT SHOP

May you celebrate this season with joy

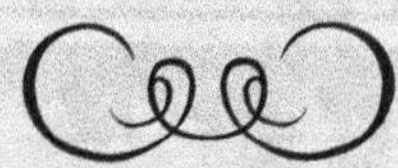

May we light up the
world with hope

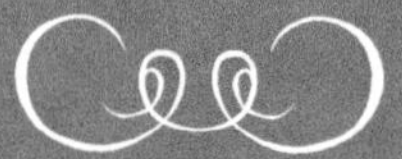

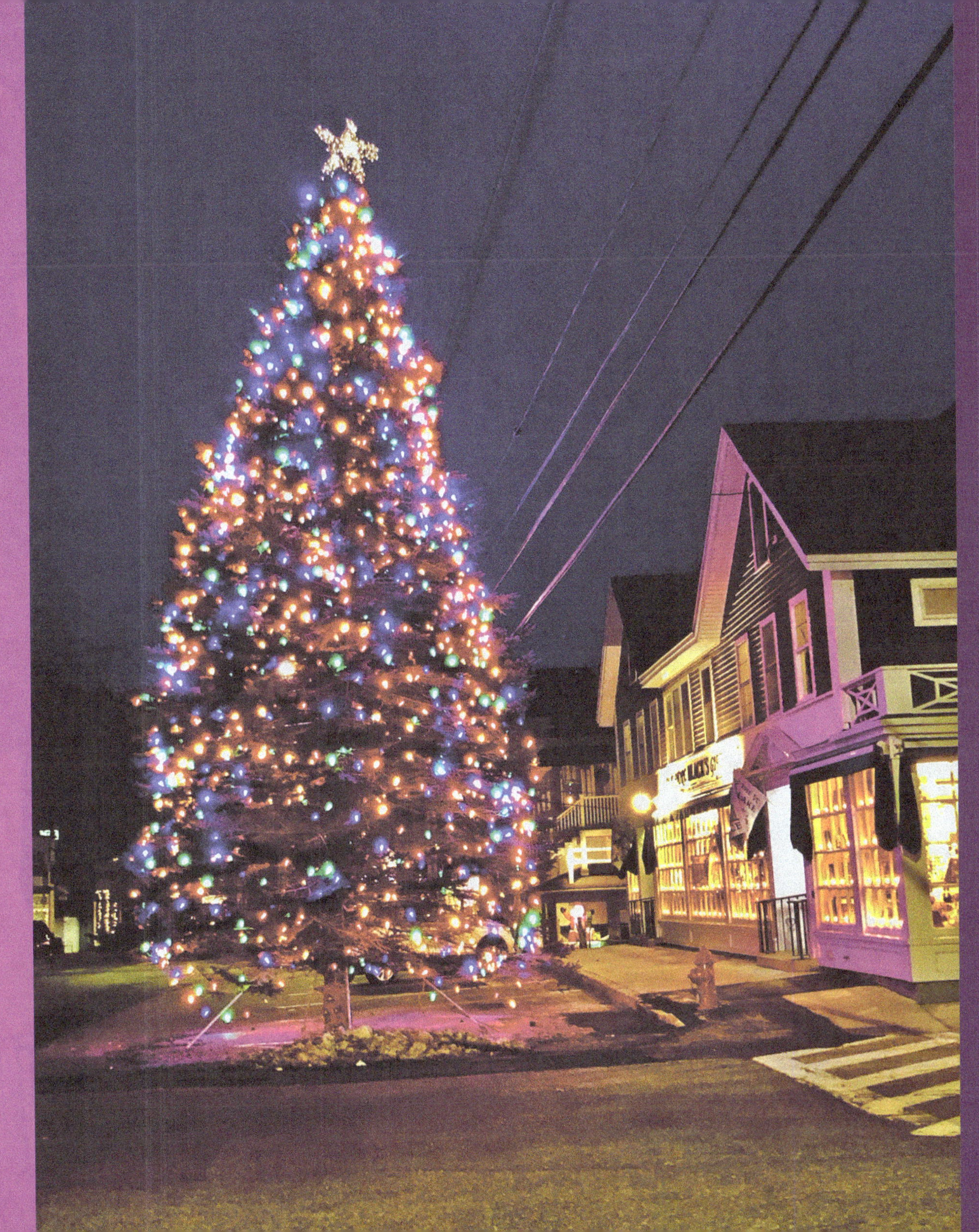

www.ingramcontent.com/pod-product-compliance
Lightning Source LLC
Chambersburg PA
CBHW080403030726
47601CB00003B/222